Llewellyn's

2019
Witches'
Companion

An Almanac for Everyday Living

Llewellyn Publications is a registered trademark of Llewellyn Worldwide Ltd.

Art Director: Lynne Menturweck
Cover art © Tim Foley
Cover designer: Lynne Menturweck
Designer: Joanna Willis
Editor: Andrea Neff

Interior illustrations:
Kathleen Edwards: 11, 14, 17, 20, 93, 96, 101, 147, 150, 178, 183, 225, 228
Tim Foley: 27, 30, 34, 105, 108, 113, 139, 142, 171, 174, 217, 220
Bri Hermanson: 48, 52, 54, 82, 86, 89, 157, 159, 197, 200, 232, 236, 239
Jennifer Hewitson: 39, 42, 69, 73, 76, 126, 128, 132, 165, 166, 205, 208, 212
Rik Olson: 59, 63, 66, 118, 123, 189, 192, 247, 250

ISBN 978-0-7387-4615-9

You can order Llewellyn annuals and books from *New Worlds*, Llewellyn's magazine catalog. To request a free copy of the catalog, call toll-free 1-877-NEW-WRLD or visit our website at www.llewellyn.com.

Llewellyn Publications
A Division of Llewellyn Worldwide Ltd.
2143 Wooddale Drive
Woodbury, MN 55125-2989
www.llewellyn.com

Printed in the United States of America

Contents

Community Forum

Provocative Opinions on Contemporary Topics

Magical Self-Care

Nurture Your Body, Mind & Spirit

Witchy Living

Day-by-Day Witchcraft

Witchcraft Essentials

Practices, Rituals & Spells

The Lunar Calendar

September 2018 to December 2019

Community Forum

Provocative Opinions on Contemporary Topics

Am I Under a Curse and What Should I Do about It?

Deborah Lipp

If you speak about magic in public—which I do from time to time—the number-one questions you are asked about curses are "Am I under a curse?" and "How do I remove the curse I presume I am under?" They are more popular even than "How do I use magic to win the lottery?"

Are You Under a Curse?

Probably not.

Recently, I appeared on a radio show, and several call-in listeners asked about curses. Caller A told the following story:

"I was in a spiritual cult. I began to realize that they were very negative and were doing curses. As I was leaving, the leader told me he would curse me if I left."

Caller B's story was this: "Lately nothing goes right. Job interviews go well, but then my husband or I [both unemployed] don't get the job. My health took a turn for the worse. I don't have any enemies that I know of, but something is wrong—could it be a curse?"

I told Caller A that yes, it sounded like she was under a curse, while I told Caller B she was not.

If you think you're under a curse, ask yourself if it's *specific*. Is there an enemy or rival who has both magical skills and a nasty interpretation of morality? Is there a particular *reason* someone has to curse you, and do they have the *ability*? If the answer to these questions is no, you're not under a curse.

There's a lot in life that can cause unfortunate circumstances. Caller B, and many thousands of people like her, could be affected by any of the following:

- **Negative behavior**—She may have herself to blame. Is her bad health due to an unhealthy diet? Are her interview skills as good as she thinks they are? Are there typos in her résumé?

- **Negative energy**—Is she poisoning herself with self-hatred, fear, or anxiety? Is it time for meditation or therapy?

- **Karma**—Is she going through dark times for a higher purpose? Is she working through something on the inner planes?

- **Messages**—Is a higher being putting obstacles in her way to get her attention?

- **Oversensitivity to energy**—Is she oversensitive to the energies around her?

- **Plain old bad luck**—Are her planets currently in a particularly difficult alignment?

It is common to attribute a bad turn of events to a curse rather than looking within (which can be painful) or shrugging it off (which can feel like a loss of control).

The truth is that I detect one person under a curse for every twenty people who come to me believing they are. It's just not that common.

What to Do about a Curse

If you believe you *are* under a curse, there are several good steps to take, and none of them will do any harm if there is no curse on you after all.

Step 1: Ignore It

All magic follows the path of least resistance, and curses are no exception. The easiest way to negatively affect people, to "curse" them, is to make them believe they're under a curse. Filling your mind with doubt and fear will undermine every aspect of your life.

I once had a breakup during which my ex did and said some horrific things to me, not to mention I found out he'd been deceiving me since the day we met. I wanted to strike back, but my own ethics restrained me. Still, when I sent him a package of things he'd left at my place, I placed in the box a piece of ginger root from my fridge.

Ginger has lots of positive magical associations; there's nothing negative about it. However, the root is gnarly and ugly and I knew it would look out of place among shirts and books. Sure enough, I got a furious email saying HE KNEW what I was up to, and HE KNEW POWERFUL PEOPLE who would protect him. I laughed like a loon.

I didn't curse my ex, but I let him think I did. I wonder if the fear and rage he experienced functioned much like a curse might have. If he'd just shrugged it off and said to himself "She can't hurt me," he'd have been fine.

If you are under a curse, shrugging it off is powerful magic. My spouse says that one of the greatest spells you can recite is "I'm rubber, you're glue. What you say bounces off me and sticks to you."

If you are under a curse, shrugging it off is powerful magic. My spouse says that one of the greatest spells you can recite is "I'm rubber, you're glue. What you say bounces off me and sticks to you." Yes, you learned that in grade school, but it still works. Laugh at your enemy. (Humor is exceptionally potent

against curses.) Acknowledge your enemy's impotence. Let the whole thing go. Very often, that's all the magic you need.

Step 2: Bless and Shield

Blessing and shielding are acts that can help you in many situations. If you're not under a curse but are having a run of bad luck, blessing and shielding will help. If you're sensitive to energy that surrounds you—because you're empathic, or because you're raw or wide open, or perhaps because you're depleted by recent or current illness, grief, or depression—then shielding protects you. There are very rare people who have the ability to "accidentally curse," people whose anger or intense emotion can actually harm others, even if they don't mean to. Shielding can protect you from that as well. And both blessing and shielding can protect you from actual curses.

If a curse is in place, blessings and shields should be applied to yourself, your home, your surroundings, and anyone who lives with you. How to do a blessing is an essay at least as long as this one, and several books on shielding are in print, so neither subject can be thoroughly covered in this article. But here are some simple steps to get you started.

To bless yourself, start in a cast circle or other sealed ritual space. Call upon the deity or deities of your choice. Ask for blessing simply and humbly. *Bless me, Mother* is a perfectly good request. See the blessing fill you. Then ask for each additional blessing (*Bless my home,* etc.) and see the blessing extend outward. When done, say *Thank you for this blessing* before closing the ritual. Then place an offering to the deity(ies) someplace outside as further thanks.

The simplest shield is an egg or aura of white pulsing light that surrounds you. I visualize it encompassing me thoroughly, from head to toe, carefully including even the soles of my feet. I like to finish by picturing negative people bouncing off of me, then picturing beloved people walking right through my shields and giving me a big hug—I don't want to be shielded against love! It's easy to be more walled-off than truly shielded, creating a situation where no one and nothing can get in. I like to imagine a shield as akin to polarized sunglasses. The UV rays can't get in, but good light can—otherwise you couldn't see.

During a period of hospitalization many years ago, I shielded every morning as soon as I woke up. I was surrounded by sick and scared people, and I needed extra protection. Some people routinely shield, and some use it to protect themselves from the ordinary intensity of life—for example, before going out into a crowd or riding the subway. If you think you're under a curse, shielding twice a day, morning and night, is called for.

Some people routinely shield, and some use it to protect themselves from the ordinary intensity of life—for example, before going out into a crowd or riding the subway. If you think you're under a curse, shielding twice a day, morning and night, is called for.

Before shielding for the first time, smudge or otherwise cleanse yourself so you don't seal in any negativity.

Again, extend the shield over your home and household.

Step 3: Cleanse, Banish, and Seal

Now we're at the "if all else fails" stage. You've determined that yes, this is a curse. You've laughed it off. You've blessed and shielded. You've let a little time pass—enough to determine if things have changed. But the effects of the curse persist.

The next thing to do is to find the source of the curse. Where is it? People often don't consider this; they treat a curse like a miasma, a nebulous state of being. But a real curse is coming from someone and directed to someone. It is getting to you somehow.

If you know who is cursing you, that person is one possible "where." However, making the magical connection necessary in order to bind that person's magic might not feel like a good idea. It's also not always possible. I once worked to remove a curse on a brother and sister—their father had been cursed, including his future children, many years before. The person who cursed their father was unknown to them and probably no longer alive.

In order to find the appropriate source of your curse, you'll need to use a combination of thought, intuition, and sixth sense. Every case is different.

Think about how the curse manifests in your life. What happens? Is there a pattern? Are events related by an idea, a specific problem area, an element, a time of day, or a moon phase? Use all your senses to explore what the curse feels, looks, sounds, smells, and tastes like.

Determine: Is this negativity (perhaps a lingering nastiness in a spot in your home), or is it a curse (which is directed from someone to you), or is it an entity of some kind? An entity would require banishment, general negativity would require cleansing, and a curse would require seals and protections. It's likely that a curse will also bring negativity, so you'd use all three: cleanse, banish, and seal.

If you're not under a curse, how did the negativity get there? Perhaps you used to be under a curse and a trace of it lingers. Perhaps you recently had someone awful around—an ex-lover, a roommate, or a burglar—and it feels like they're still there. I had a friend who inherited an office from a screaming, angry person. I did a cleansing for her on her first day in the new office. Cleansing and banishing can go hand in hand so that the aura of the curse doesn't stay behind when the curse is blocked.

Determine: Is this negativity (perhaps a lingering nastiness in a spot in your home), or is it a curse (which is directed from someone to you), or is it an entity of some kind? An entity would require banishment, general negativity would require cleansing, and a curse would require seals and protections.

In a number of cases I've simply walked through a location using my hands to explore what each part of the room felt like. Pay attention to openings: doors, windows, vents, faucets, drains. Notice thresholds: transitions from one space to another. Does the energy change in different areas? Does one room or one access point create negative feelings? In one instance it was quite obvious to me that water, in any location, felt more negative. Sinks and toilets gave off a nasty aura. This gave me an understanding of where the curse was coming from.

Once you know where the problem is coming from, you can banish, cleanse, and/or seal. Spells that accomplish this will vary widely based on individual circumstances, although the basic structure is simple. For example, when choosing an incense, you might go for cleansing, purification, power, banishment, etc. The more powerful the banishing incense, the more likely it is to stink. Asafoetida, for example, is noxious. You would use this strongest-possible incense only if you really had to; it's akin to having an exterminator come in—the smell can be bad enough and the chemical poisonous enough to force you to move out for a few days.

Stopping the Person Directly

If you choose this method, you are stopping the person who is cursing you from doing so; more specifically, you're stopping the curse from reaching you. This is effective only if a curse is being actively sent to work against you, or will be in the future. You can use the following method to prevent your enemy from renewing the curse.

1. Work in a cast circle or other protected ritual space.

2. Gather your usual magical power tool (athame, wand, etc.), an image or symbol of your enemy, a clear drinking glass or two small mirrors or a mirror compact (mirrored on both sides), and a tray of some kind to keep the whole apparatus on.

3. Burn a strong purifying incense such as frankincense.

4. Point your tool at the symbol of your enemy, saying *You are (name of enemy)*.

5. Seal your enemy's negativity by placing the glass over the symbol of your enemy, or by placing the symbol between the two mirrors (with the reflecting surface facing in) or inside the mirrored compact. (I buy small mirrors, one to four inches square, at craft supply stores. They have lots of magical uses.)

6. Say: *Your curse is sealed in and cannot escape. You can do no harm, no harm can escape.*

7. Sending all your power, say *You can do no harm* over and over until you feel the power release.

8. Say: *So be it.*

9. Leave your sealed enemy on the tray in a dark place as long as you think is necessary. Be prepared to leave it there permanently.

Cleansing/Banishing/Sealing

The following steps can be used to accomplish these three goals. The water dishes are for cleansing, the incense is for both cleansing and banishing, the banishing pentagrams are for banishing, the use of a magical tool and spoken words is for all three goals, and the invoking pentagrams at the end are for sealing.

By now, you've determined the source of the problem, and this will control where the spell is done, what element(s) are used, what kind of incense is used, and the exact wording. The following spell is a generic version using all the doors and windows of a home.

1. You'll need your magical power tool (athame, wand, etc.), a bottle or pitcher of pure spring water, a set of bowls or dishes, and burning incense. It might be convenient to set the empty bowls out in advance at each location before you begin.

2. If there are multiple locations, you'll be going around the house, stopping at each. For doors, always start at the front door, and go around the house widdershins (counterclockwise).

3. At the front door, make a banishing pentagram with your magical tool, saying the following (rewrite these words to be specific to your situation):

I *banish all evil that has entered through this door by the power of (God/the Goddess/My guardian angel/My true will, etc., as you see fit). This door is safe, and evil cannot enter here. I cleanse and purify this door that it is a fit passageway. So be it.*

The elements involved will determine what kind of banishing pentagram to use. If no elemental involvement is detected, use an earth banishing pentagram.

4. Cense the door thoroughly, starting at the bottom right, going around counterclockwise, and ending where you began. Repeat the same words.

5. Leave a dish of water by the door.

6. Repeat this procedure for every door and window in the home. One dish of water per room is usually enough, unless it's a huge room with many doors and windows.

7. When you've done the whole house, go back around, this time clockwise. Make an invoking pentagram (of the same element as the banishing pentagram used earlier) at each door and window, saying:

I do seal this door, by the power of (as before), that only good can enter herein. So be it.

8. Leave the water dishes out overnight. In the morning, get rid of all the water. It should be poured out onto the earth but not on your own property. The dishes should then be thoroughly cleansed in very hot water. (They can be run through the dishwasher.)

STEP 4: ADD PROTECTION

Once you've acted on the curse—by ignoring it, by blessing/shielding, or by cleansing, banishing, and sealing—you should do the additional step of protecting yourself and your home magically.

Many people have simple protection spells on their homes as a matter of course, perhaps using a floor wash on the front steps, hanging a witch ball, placing a protective charm under the doormat, or burying a witches' bottle. Once you've removed a curse, you should certainly place such protection as a guard for the future. The following is a simple example of a protection spell for a home.

Many people have simple protection spells on their homes as a matter of course, perhaps using a floor wash on the front steps, hanging a witch ball, placing a protective charm under the doormat, or burying a witches' bottle.

1. Gather your magical power tool (athame, wand, etc.), four small mirrors, and symbols of the four elements: incense, a candle, a dish of water, and a dish of salt.

2. Point your tool at the mirrors, saying:

I *charge these mirrors with protection, that they serve as guardians. No evil can pass them. Return, return, return, O evil, whence you came!*

3. Pass the mirrors through the incense smoke, saying:

By *the power of air do* I *charge these mirrors with protection. Return, return, return, O evil!*

4. Repeat for the element of fire as you pass the mirrors through the flame, water as you wet the mirrors, and earth as you rub salt on the mirrors. Be sure the mirrors are thoroughly imbued with each element. End with *So be it!*

5. Bury one mirror at each of the cardinal points (east, south, west, north) of your property. They should be facing out, so that evil coming from outside your property is reflected back at the intruder.

．．．．．．．．．．．．

Despite what many people think about Witchcraft and magic, curses are quite rare. Nonetheless, they do exist, and smart practitioners of magic should know how to protect themselves!

Deborah Lipp *is the author of eight books, including* Magical Power For Beginners: How to Raise & Send Energy for Spells That Work, Tarot Interactions: Become More Intuitive, Psychic & Skilled at Reading Cards, *and* Merry Meet Again: Lessons, Life & Love on the Path of a Wiccan High Priestess. *Deborah has been Wiccan for most of her life and a High Priestess of the Gardnerian tradition for the past thirty years. She's been published in* newWitch, Llewellyn's Magical Almanac, Pangaia, *and* Green Egg. *Deborah lives in Jersey City with her spouse, Melissa, and an assortment of cats.*

Illustrator: Kathleen Edwards

Blogs, Books, Columns, and Essays: How to Write for the Pagan Marketplace

Susan Pesznecker

In today's digital age, the processes of writing, sharing, and publishing are simpler and widely available to all of us. But this doesn't mean the actual act of writing is any easier. In this article, I'm hoping to separate the writing process into a set of thoughtful steps, showing you ways to combine creativity and organization to craft a solid written piece.

Get Ready

Before you start, think about when and where you'll write. We all have times of day when we feel sharp and creative, so capitalize on that. Be selfish in carving out dedicated time for writing, and pick the right place, too, whether that means a location that's perfectly quiet or one full of people and noise. Choose your writing tools with equal care.

Intention

When starting any writing project, it's a good idea to reflect on what you're creating. For instance, are you …

- planning to write a blog?

- creating a website for your writing?

- submitting an article or essay to a Pagan magazine?

- writing just for yourself, as in a personal journal?

Consider that every piece of writing is unique, with its own focus, tone, and specific structure. For instance, a magazine article proceeds in linear fashion from one point to another and reaches a climax and conclusion, while a journal is a set of personal and emotional reflections or observations. Thinking about this in advance will help guide you as your writing takes shape, giving you a sense of focus and an endpoint to shoot for.

Know Your Audience

In addition to having a vision of the finished piece, it's important to think about your audience. Who are they? Are your readers new to the Craft or established elders? Will variables such as age, gender, spiritual path, life experience, and home location affect the way a reader reacts to your writing? These sorts of variables will affect the complexity of your piece, the language it uses, and its scope.

Your audience will also help determine the tone of the piece—that is, the way it establishes a certain mood or feel. Depending on what you're writing, the tone might be supportive, instructive, angry, rebellious, or even sarcastic. Consider the difference in tone in these two paragraphs about working with binding spells:

1. Binding spells are dark and fraught with danger. Even in experienced hands, they may be perilous. Worst-case scenario: they can backfire and rebound catastrophically. Be aware, be fearful, and protect yourself.

2. Are you interested in working with binding spells? As a beginner, be aware that these spells must be performed thoughtfully and with care. It's best to do a lot of research before you begin. Even better, study and learn the process with an experienced teacher, and then proceed slowly, one step at a time.

Notice the difference in tone? The first one has short, clipped sentences and uses words designed to sound intimidating. The second has longer, more flowing sentences with words chosen to emphasize learning and confidence.

Publication

If you're hoping to have your work published, you'll either (a) self-publish or (b) work with a publisher.

Self-Publishing

This route is what most people choose, as it's easy and the quickest way to get one's work into print. Blogging is one kind of self-publishing, as is populating your own website or writing fanfiction. A number of services allow you to publish your work in e-book or hard-copy formats, and many Pagan publications accept articles, hire columnists, or even take on journalists for actual reporting work. If you want to go this route, do good research and ask for input from people using various services.

Working with a Publisher

This option, while still important, is becoming ever more difficult. Because of the exploding popularity of self-publishing, publishers are now a lot more selective about which works they agree to publish, and the process has become extremely competitive. If you wish to submit to a publisher, look for one that handles Pagan-type works. Consult their website for submission information, and do exactly what is requested. Be aware that your work is much more likely to be turned down by professional publishers than accepted, and if your work is accepted, you'll be following precise guidelines, working with editors, and making editing and content changes to the work. You'll be contracted, binding you to a firm agreement and giving you less freedom. All of that aside, working with a publisher is exciting and can open doors to future work.

Getting Inspired

I always suggest beginning with "invention," an activity that uses brainstorming to warm up and get the creative juices flowing. Some writers like to start with lists, while others prefer to draw mind maps.

Some writers like to start with lists, while others prefer to draw mind maps. An easy way for everyone to begin is with freewriting. Using your topic as a prompt, set a timer for 5–10 minutes, and during that time, write down everything you already know or believe about your topic. Write down questions, too.

An easy way for everyone to begin is with freewriting. Using your topic as a prompt, set a timer for 5–10 minutes, and during that time, write down everything you already know or believe about your topic. Write down questions, too. Try to keep going without stopping, writing whatever comes to mind and not stopping to edit or correct yourself.

Once the time is up, look over your newly generated ideas and make a list of the key points you want to address in your piece and the major questions you'll need to answer before writing. Look for gaps that need to be filled. Start developing an overall vision of where the piece is headed.

Doing Research

Once you have an idea of what you want to write, it's time for research. Instead of starting with Google, look for reliable websites in the field you're covering. When you can, focus on those from .edu or .gov sites—they're always more authoritative than .com or .org sites. Even better, visit your local library or college library (most of which are open to the public), where you can access the most current books and professional publications.

In academic terms, the best reference materials are those written by experts: people with degrees, experience, or credentials in that field. This is sometimes tricky to discern in Pagan publications, because some practitioners create unique titles for themselves that sound official but actually mask their inexperience. Others may add degree credentials to their name (e.g., MA, PhD) that come from

non-university courses; these may or may not be authoritative and call for additional investigation. Bottom line: if you can't convince yourself that an author is a reliable expert, toss the source and keep exploring.

As you research, keep track of each source you refer to; e.g., record the title, author's name, web address, publisher, and so forth. You'll need this information in order to list the source materials you used.

Structuring Your Piece

The typical essay, article, or blog piece follows a traditional structure. Of course, you don't have to follow this schema, but it's the "old reliable," and it works pretty well.

1. Start with an **introduction** to let the reader know what you'll be sharing. But no "announcements," please! In other words, don't say "I will talk about the history and significance of the besom." That's boring, honestly, and it makes the reader feel like they're about to be lectured to. Instead, make clear definitive statements, like "The besom is an important magickal tool with a fascinating history." That leaves the reader intrigued and wanting more.

2. Create a set of **body paragraphs**, each one covering one point you want to make. If you start talking about a new or different idea, start a new paragraph, and start each one with a topic sentence, i.e., a sentence that introduces that paragraph's main idea. Aim for nice, juicy paragraphs that are 5–8 sentences in length.

3. **Cite your source materials.** If you use a source, you must note it in your piece. This accomplishes two goals: one, it points your reader toward additional materials, and two, it gives credit to the original author (and if you don't do that, you're technically committing plagiarism!). Plagiarism is what

happens when people use ideas or intellectual property created by someone else and don't give them credit. It's a kind of theft, it's unprofessional, and it absolutely must be avoided.

If you're writing for a publisher or publication, they may prefer a specific citation style. For example, CMS style is preferred by many publishers for books and journals, while AP style is used in magazines and newspapers. Otherwise, the simplest way to cite is to include the author's name in parentheses at the end of any sentence that contains source material, like this (Pesznecker). I've also included resources for MLA (Modern Language Association) format in the sources at the end of this article. The MLA style is the style of the humanities, which include writing, literature, philosophy, and religion. It's a good basic style, and the various Pagan practices seem to me to fit nicely within it.

4. Design your written piece so that the **most interesting moment** happens about two-thirds to three-fourths of the way through, and build up gradually to that point. This type of structure mirrors what happens in a story, with the gradual climb to a climactic point. It will be easily understood and followed by your reader.

5. **Finish with a conclusion.** And please don't just restate your main idea and main points! Instead, leave the reader feeling curious and engaged. Offer a reflection, make a prediction, finish with an important quote, or in some other way leave them thinking about your ideas.

6. **Add a list of sources** used in the piece, listing them in alphabetical order. For best results, create this list as you go; i.e., any time you insert a piece of source material into your piece, stop and add it to your sources list, too. This will help avoid the situation where a writer forgets which fact came from which source.

7. At some point in the process, **add a title.** You may have a great title before you even begin, or you may find your title as you write. An old writer's trick is to find your favorite sentence in the written piece and use that to create a title. However you accomplish it, your title should always inform the reader of what's coming. If it can also be clever, so much the better.

Do you have to work through these seven steps in order? Absolutely not. I, for one, can't write an introduction until I have some of my body paragraphs done. And I may suddenly come up with a great conclusion when the writing is only halfway finished. Figure out what kind of forward process works for you and follow it. Rules, schmules.

Controversy and Thick Skin

As your writing takes shape, go back and think again about your own intentions, and be even more aware of the audience you're writing for.

Understand clearly that no matter how brilliant your writing and how clear your ideas, you're likely to have haters, for want of a better term. Disagreement and argument seem to be the rule for reading, writing, and discussion in the various Pagan (and related) practices.

And then, once you've done that, understand clearly that no matter how brilliant your writing and how clear your ideas, you're likely to have haters, for want of a better term. Disagreement and argument seem to be the rule for reading, writing, and discussion in the various Pagan (and related) practices, and the more controversial your ideas, the more pushback you're likely to experience. Part of

this is because Pagan folk tend to be educated, articulate, and feisty, but another factor is the ongoing disagreement between "big tent" ideas and those on the periphery. The discourse is made easier in the online setting, where it's almost impossible to avoid discussions.

If you've written a sound piece—one that's carefully researched, uses strong sources, and has all sources cited—you can be confident that you've done your job well. And once you know that, simply accept (and expect!) that your readers' opinions will vary. Some will love you, but others may disagree vehemently, raise uncomfortable questions, or even say something unkind. This is simply part of the reality of writing for the public. Engage in discussion as you choose to, avoid discussions you really don't want to participate in, and use your <DELETE> function to take care of the trolls.

Writing in Drafts

I strongly suggest that you write in a series of drafts. Writing teachers and those who study the craft of writing know that this is the best way to produce a really effective piece of written work. What does it mean to write in drafts?

FIRST DRAFT

After you've finished your freewriting, created a simple structure for your piece, and done some good research, you're ready to create a first draft. Your goal here is to build on the simple structure you've written. Don't try to be precise or even organized; simply get the ideas from your head onto the page. One of my writing professors called this "word vomit." Just let it go! Only when your ideas and content are on the page can you begin the process of fine-tuning.

In my writing classes I use this example to explain the process: To make a beautiful vase, you have to start with raw, wet clay and probably also a simple diagram of the vase. You lug the mass of clay to your work space and plop it on the table. Only after the clay is there can the vase take shape. No clay, no vase! As a writer, your freewriting is like the mass of clay, and your basic, simple structure is like the diagram of the vase. Creating the basic vase is your first draft. Simply said, your writing can't begin until you have generated ideas to work with.

Once your draft is on paper, it's time to go through and rewrite sentences, add sources, and so forth. Then, I strongly suggest you tuck the draft away for a couple of days or even a week or two. No peeking! Leave it untouched for that period of time, and when you open it later, you'll be surprised at how fresh it looks to you.

SECOND DRAFT

Start by reading the piece aloud. Trust me: by reading aloud, you'll hear errors and clunky spots that your eyes won't see. It's probably the most effective way to review a piece of one's own writing.

Make any changes, edits, or additions that seem needed. At this point, make sure your piece has a good introduction and conclusion and an interesting title. Add a sources list, if you haven't already.

Now for something very important: your **first reader**. A first reader is someone who will read your writing and give you honest feedback. Give them a clean copy and a pen to jot down questions, write in the margins, etc. Ask them to read the piece and write down anything that comes to mind, errors, and so forth. Tell them to be merciless. Promise them cookies. And respect their comments.

Can you do more than two drafts? Absolutely. Lather, rinse, and repeat—your writing will keep getting better.

Editing and GUSP

Use your first reader's comments to edit and polish your draft. Make sure the grammar, usage, spelling, and punctuation (GUSP) are absolutely correct: there's no way to lose a reader faster than with simple errors like these. Thankfully, there are wonderful resources online to help shine up your piece.

Backups!

Finally, be sure to back up your work from your computer, i.e., on a thumb drive, via cloud storage, or whatever works for you. Your computer is only a machine and one day it will die, and if you haven't saved your work elsewhere, it will be lost.

. . . .

Fellow writer, if you follow at least some of these suggestions, I feel confident that you'll produce a wonderful piece of writing—one that you can be proud of and one that has something to say to your magickal colleagues. Well done, you!

Recommended Materials

Babin, Monique, Carol Burnell, Susan Pesznecker, Nicole Rosevear, and Jaime Wood. *The Word on College Reading and Writing.* Open Oregon Educational Resources, 2017. https://openoregon.pressbooks.pub/wrd.

The MLA Style Center. Modern Language Association of America. https://style.mla.org.

Pesznecker, Susan. *Crafting Magick with Pen and Ink.* Woodbury, MN: Llewellyn, 2009.

Susan Pesznecker *is a mother, writer, nurse, college English teacher, and Baden-Powell Service Association scout and lives in the beautiful Pacific Northwest with her poodles. An initiated Druid, green magick devoteé, and amateur herbalist, Sue loves reading, writing, cooking, travel, camping, swimming, stargazing, and anything having to do with the outdoors. Her previous books include* Crafting Magick with Pen and Ink, The Magickal Retreat: Making Time for Solitude, Intention & Rejuvenation, *and* Yule: Recipes & Lore for the Winter Solstice. *She is also a regular contributor to the Llewellyn annuals. Follow her at www.facebook.com/SusanMoonwriterPesznecker.*

Illustrator: Tim Foley

A Witch's Guide to Essential Etiquette

Laura Tempest Zakroff

Etiquette may seem like an old-fashioned concept to discuss, but being aware of how to interact with others is essential to building a healthy community and developing your own personal practice.

So many people nowadays are introduced to the path of the Witch through books and solitary studies. For the most part, it is a wonderful thing that this type of information is more accessible than ever. It used to be that you had to find a coven or similar kind of group near you to learn from. But there is a drawback: details regarding interpersonal

relationships and interactions are not covered in books, whether introductory or advanced. It can also be difficult to navigate social nuances through online courses. It's so easy to lose the immediacy of human reactions as we make contact in cyberspace.

Another thing to consider is that we're wading through a new age of religious and spiritual structure. Few of the religious paths that folks may originate from give much applicable guidance or structure when it comes to defining clergy, creating spaces, and dealing with issues that are specific to Witchcraft. There is no one holy scripture to dictate moral guidelines, ethics, and professional standards. For example, the Wiccan Rede may be followed by some Wiccans, but it isn't embraced by all varieties of Witches, including myself. There are numerous codes, keys, oaths, and tenets—as many as there are traditions, if not more!

So how does etiquette help us? Whether you look at Witchcraft as a religion, a spiritual path, a vocation, a way of life, a method, a tool, or a mixture of all of these, the practice of etiquette applies to you. Let's consider the definition of the word itself. Google Dictionary tells us that etiquette is *the customary code of polite behavior in society or among members of a particular profession or group.* No matter if we practice alone or in a group, coven, or church, social and professional guidelines help us create standards to hold ourselves to and aid us when working with anyone from any path. Etiquette can be the stars to guide our ships in fair weather, as well as the wind that moves us through difficult situations. It also helps us avoid situations that can be embarrassing or damaging. Or, at the least, it can aid us in recovering gracefully when we do make a mistake—which we are all inclined to do at some point!

The following guidelines are rules of etiquette that I follow and teach to my students. It's not an easy path (another reason why it is often called the crooked path!), but these tips can make your journey smoother and less stressful. They're also good for keeping your broom from being chewed on by the drama llama!

Your Word Is Your Worth

As Witches, we work with a lot of seemingly intangible things, such as spirits, deities, magick, and metaphysics. However, we know they are real from our own experiences. You should likewise consider what you say and what you write as also being real and having an impact. Words contain a lot of power, so they must be used wisely.

Be true to your word. If you cannot keep a promise or keep to your word, don't lie. Instead, be direct and considerate. Avoid trying to appease others and making empty commitments when you know you can't follow through. It's better to be upfront and disappoint others at the get-go than to build up deception over time. You'll forge much healthier relationships and have a lot less stress that way.

Don't Piss on the Seedlings—They Become Trees

Value everyone you come across and treat them with respect, whether you know who they are or not. Often, amazing power can come from the most unassuming of packages, especially if given a chance to thrive.

Value everyone you come across and treat them with respect, whether you know who they are or not. Often, amazing power can come from the most unassuming of packages, especially if given a chance to thrive. Community is built by recognizing the importance of *all* of the generations and cycles.

Community is built by recognizing the importance of *all* of the generations and cycles. Far too often we make assumptions about people we don't know based on appearance, gender, age, or experience. Dismissing someone as an unimportant "weed," as uninformed or inexperienced, because you're not familiar with them will only get you in trouble down the line. We know as Witches that a lot of important magick can come from sources dismissed as mere weeds. In the garden we know that tending to seedlings with enough patience and care can produce amazing plants. Plus, we all have to start somewhere and we each have our own pace of learning and growth. Practicing mutual respect grows a healthy and diverse forest.

Speaking of Trees, They All Can Be Felled

No one is too tall, too mighty, too strong, too powerful, or impervious. There are always storms and forest fires, disease can come in many forms, and the ground underneath the tree may erode away. Essentially, no one is greater or better than anyone else. Even the seemingly smallest thing can cause something big to crash down. It's important to practice self-respect, but don't make the mistake of considering yourself more important than anyone or anything else. Trying to garner favor and power by threatening or bullying others is unhealthy and unnecessary—and a waste of energy that could be used instead to do something beneficial. Overestimating your power or pull can also get you in a lot of trouble metaphysically, potentially causing harm to yourself and others mentally, physically, and/or spiritually. Be confident, but practice humility and self-awareness, and you'll have a solid foundation.

The Same Plant Can Heal or Harm
Depending on How You Interact with It

Nothing is entirely "good" or "evil." Some incredibly helpful plants are invasive, while others have poisonous blooms but tasty roots. Some prickly plants provide homes for endangered birds.

Keep this same wisdom in mind regarding people. I am friends with a great variety of people, and some of those friends do not get along with others. I hear and acknowledge the differences of opinion and the problems, but I also recognize the strengths and positive attributes too. Just because someone disagrees with you on one topic doesn't make them evil—likewise for the inverse. It's far safer to understand nuances than to decree that everything must be absolute.

Cultivating a variety of people in your life who have different backgrounds and ideas is a beautiful thing. It prevents you from becoming ensconced in an echo chamber and breaks the comfortable bubbles we tend to float in. Differing opinions and points of view can stimulate new ideas and perspectives while also honing our problem-solving skills.

However, I'm *not* saying you have to tolerate people in your life who can be harmful through their words and actions. But it can be very beneficial to familiarize yourself with them peripherally. I have foxglove, nightshade, and hemlock growing naturally in my yard, but only the lavender, rosemary, and mint are allowed inside. Take this same approach with people: identify their nature, recognize their good and bad traits, and work with what is best for your needs. You don't have to drink the poison that others dish out.

Don't Poison the Cauldron

Speaking of beneficial and baneful traits, hold a mirror to yourself, your intentions, and your actions. Are you intentionally causing harm without reason? I'm all for hexing to bring justice, binding to contain a situation, and other forms of what can be considered baneful magick, but attacking others in your community out of spite or for perceived slights—through magick or words—is irresponsible. It may soothe your ego temporarily, but you do reap what you sow. Remember, we're all interconnected on so many levels, and even more so in non-mainstream cultures such as the paths under the Pagan umbrella. We have far more in common than we are different. If you purposefully pour poison into the well you drink from, eventually you will feel the effects.

What's Good for the Goose Is What's Good for the Goose

When someone states "This is how I do things" or "This is how it works for me," that's exactly what they are saying. They are not saying your way is wrong or invalid—unless they are saying precisely that as well. (Example: "This is the way that works, and your way sucks/is wrong." That makes that person a jerk, and the validity of their opinion is likely suspect.)

The path of the Witch requires developing trust in your intuition and forging your own journey. You are your own pioneer, so your path is going to be unique to your own world. Because there is no one standard to go by, many practitioners fall prey to insecurity, worrying that they might not be doing it right or are missing something vital.

It's natural to compare and contrast, but don't create competition or drama where it doesn't exist. It's exhausting to always be on the defensive, and even more so when you don't need to be. You're not sure what someone means? Ask them to clarify, *politely*. Don't read into something that's not there.

Follow the Intent

Similarly, it is wise to watch and be aware of your baggage. If someone verbally missteps with a word or phrase, take a moment to consider what they really are trying to say. Rather than immediately getting defensive, going on the offensive, or being triggered, take a moment to reflect. What is causing this response in you? Is there something in your past bubbling up, a pattern or a behavior?

Communication happens in many ways and at multiple levels, including listening, processing, speaking, nonverbal cues, posture, tone, etc.—much of which can be extremely difficult to suss out online or if someone communicates differently from you. Ask yourself: Do they mean well or did they intend to harm? Is there a better and more productive way to address the issue? Is this the time or place for a teaching moment? Is the situation more conducive to calling in versus calling out? How would you feel if you were in their boots? Lastly, if it's happening online, try to envision having the same experience face to face. (This guideline is courtesy of my dear friend Anaar.)

Threefold Literacy

Witches absorb, think, then act. This behavior should apply to all things, especially the internet. As I mentioned earlier, the Wiccan Rede, and particularly the Rule of Three, isn't part of my path. But I do like the number three and have a guideline centered on it in regard to correspondence. My rule of three is this: Read everything three times before choosing a course of action. Similarly, I read my response three times before entering/sending it. This rule gives you time to absorb and make sure you understand what you're reading, and eliminates most confusing or reactionary elements. It also allows you to beat the sinister demon of the internet: autocorrect.

Those Who Show Up Determine the Outcome— There Is No Absentee Ballot in Witchcraft

It's amazing what people complain about, especially when it comes to events and happenings of a community nature. When there's a problem trying to be solved, I constantly see people saying "That's why I don't do X/participate in the community," and then they fail to present any sort of solution. It's ridiculously easy to criticize, but it's far more difficult to actually get up and do something about the problem. Words that aren't followed up with action lose power. Don't like the way something is run? Volunteer, offer assistance, or bring into existence your own vision if you dare. Community is created by those who show up. If you're willing to raise your voice and want to see change happen, you should also be prepared to follow through by actively participating and being present to the best of your ability.

. . . .

So those are nine guidelines to prevent Witch wars, foster community, and create a balanced path of living Witchcraft. We all make mistakes, but we can always try to do better. Be kind to yourself, and extend the same courtesy to others while co-experiencing this beautiful life. Go forth and manifest birches!

Laura Tempest Zakroff *can be described as a professional artist, author, dancer, designer, muse, mythpunk, teacher, and Witch. She has been a practicing Modern Traditional Witch for over two decades and revels in the intersection of her various paths. She blogs for Patheos as* A Modern Traditional Witch *and for Witches &Pagans as* Fine Art Witchery. *She is the author of* The Witch's Cauldron: The Craft, Lore & Magick of Ritual Vessels *and* Sigil Witchery: A Witch's Guide to Crafting Magick Symbols, *and co-authored* The Witch's Altar *with Jason Mankey. Laura resides in Seattle and can be found online at www.lauratempestzakroff.com.*

Illustrator: Jennifer Hewitson

Getting in the Flow of Magickal Work

Raven Digitalis

We all know the phrase *getting in the flow*. It has an encouraging tone, one lacking stress and boosting confidence. Unlike *going with* the flow, which tends to be passive, *getting in* the flow implies action and involvement. When it comes to magickal work and spiritual work, this is a must: we must be in a deeper creative flow than usual in order to create, manifest, and project our intentions into reality.

As spiritual artists, we co-create and build our experiences of reality through intentional magickal work and through our daily thoughts and actions. Spiritual

rituals of all varieties—including life itself—rely primarily on the practitioner.

Our attitudes and approaches are the most important components of our work. Regardless of how many sigils we draw, how many deities we call forth, and how rare the ingredients are that we use in a spell, the success of our work depends primarily on *ourselves* as the crafters, the architects.

As I sit down to write this article, I feel a certain confidence in creating the piece. I am in the flow. For that reason, this article comes easily. It flows; it's not forced. The words write themselves, and I am merely the conduit. The same holds true for other works of art and for works of magick. Besides, is there really a difference between the two? The illustrious, revolutionary, and ever-controversial occultist Aleister Crowley once said that all magick is art. As all artists know, art cannot be forced; the same goes for magickal work! We can try to force it, sometimes successfully, but the most successful and least stressful method of creation is to get in the flow to see where—and how—we are taken.

What Is the Flow?

Energetic flow occurs when we feel aligned, balanced, and confident. This makes a huge difference in our intentional work and in our lives in general. But it's not always easy to get to this place. There are times when life sucks—or at least appears to suck. Life can be dreadfully stressful, amazingly beautiful, and everything in between. Even when we are sad or stressed, we can count on life to pick us back up and align us once again with that spiral flow that assures us everything is all right. From this mental and spiritual state, we can intuitively feel that everything is happening for a reason and that we are exactly where we are supposed to be. From this place, a sense of universal trust, compassion, and spiritual connectedness has a chance to develop and flourish.

Everyone has a baseline personality, and this baseline can change with time. It's a noble goal to work both for personal happiness and for the happiness of others. If, however, you feel that your baseline personality is attached to ongoing fear, anxiety, sorrow, and pain, or if you experience extreme highs coupled with extreme lows, I encourage you with all my heart to seek counseling, therapy, and even prescription medication from a local mental health clinic (many of which even work for free or on a sliding scale). Life is much too short to live in a perpetual state of darkness, and we *all* deserve the healing it takes to reach a general baseline of happiness in life.

Reactions and Responses

Our responses to life's challenges are what define our energetic state. If we live in a constant state of stress, agitation, or depression, we are certainly not in the flow. And while it's rare that a person can remain in a perpetual state of confident bliss, everyone has moments of "okayness" and universal connectedness to varying degrees. These are the moments to take advantage of, magically and creatively.

The brain is an intricate piece of equipment, processing both subtle and complex information at speeds that surpass even the world's greatest supercomputer. Our minds are capable of feats that we may never fully understand. Metaphysical practitioners recognize the mind's connection not only to physical senses but also to the psychic world, the spirit world, the dream world, past lives, and genetic memory. The list is endless, and we find our perceptions continually returning to the eternal moment of now.

So where are you now? As you read this article and others in this book, is your mind wandering to other things, or do you feel pretty focused and in the moment? Do you feel connected, engaged, comfortable, at ease, and single-minded? If so, consider yourself in the flow and totally receptive to the information on these pages—and the dance of life around you. If your mind is currently

> **As you read this article and others in this book, is your mind wandering to other things, or do you feel pretty focused and in the moment? Do you feel connected, engaged, comfortable, at ease, and single-minded? If so, consider yourself in the flow.**

wandering or stressing about other things, then you're not quite in the moment. But with a bit of intentional focus, this can change.

We must learn to train our minds. Our thought processes are intricately linked to our emotions. Both of these things are linked to our past experiences, primarily in this lifetime but undoubtedly in past ones as well. As we react to life's various experiences, it's essential to examine the reasons behind our responses. What is the basis for our mood at any given moment? The more frequently we choose to step back from our thoughts and emotions, the more clearly we can view ourselves. The more frequently we can simply observe life without dramatically emotionalizing even the smallest things, the deeper we grow in self-awareness. Self-awareness and mindfulness help us get in the groove of positivity, lending immeasurable strength to our magickal lives and our works at hand.

The Cosmic Dance

Most Witches reading this book are undoubtedly familiar with Starhawk's Witchcraft-revival classic *The Spiral Dance*. Affirmed in this groundbreaking book is the fact that everything in life is constantly in flux. Nature's spiral dance is reflected in the cycles of the sun, the moon, and the planets, and in the cycle of birth, life, death, and rebirth. We dance the spiral of life in everything from hunting to ceremony to social interaction. All around us and within us is life's spiral dance. Dancing the spiral can be considered a core practice of our Craft.

When we are in the flow, we are flowing with life. Moreover, we are dancing with life much like India's Lord Shiva in his aspect of *Nataraj*. As one of the most common aspects of Hinduism's alchemical god Lord Shiva (also called Rudra, Mahadeva, etc.), Nataraj is seen as an emblem of the perfect Lord of the Dance.

Like all Vedic gods, goddesses, and devas, Shiva Nataraj is depicted in a manner that is rich with symbolism in order to both convey the deity's qualities and provide a focal point for devotees. Indeed, Hinduism is a mystical, magickal, and ancient path of wisdom!

Nataraj is portrayed within a burning ring of fire (A*gni*) and also holds a lick of flame in his left hand; this symbolizes the god's alignment with life's nature of change, often termed "destruction." However, Nataraj stands atop a lotus pedestal, representing life's perpetual experience of rebirth. Directly under his right foot we see him "taming," or overcoming, what is often called "the demon of ignorance." A snake (N*aga*) coils around his waist (representing *shakti/kundalini* power). He wears the clothing of an ascetic (*sadhu*), signifying the power of renouncing worldly attachments. He is depicted holding a damaru drum to represent the constant rhythm of life. His hands and feet are depicted in significant postures and mudras, and the holy river Ganges flows outward from his dreadlocked hair.

Shiva is regarded as the ideal yogi, swami, and *Brahmachari* (renunciant). In his avatar of Nataraj, he is the perfect spiral dancer who is entirely in the flow of evolution and awareness. In this aspect, Nataraj is not preoccupied, is not distracted, and is not anything but present. By performing his *dharma* (or "True Will," as a Thelemite might say), Shiva Nataraj is very much in the flow of life and existence. We can call upon Shiva and other blissfully enlightened deities in order to help ourselves remain in the flow of life, devoted to equilibrium.

Reflections on Infinity

Let's get abstract for a moment. We humans do not have the capacity to fully understand the concept of *infinity*. But infinity is a real thing, verified by science and mysticism alike. Generally we think about the infinite nature of time and space when we contemplate this concept. However, infinity is much deeper than this, penetrating every moment, every cell, every above and every below. We, as humans existing with these limited sensory capabilities, cannot accurately feel, experience, or comprehend infinity unless we invoke this experience through mind-altering, mystical, and gnostic activities such as deep meditation, trance dancing, the safe use of certain drugs, and so on.

In terms of normal-functioning consciousness, we need to find ourselves grounded and centered in any given moment. To survive *this* paradigm of experience, we must stay anchored to the present moment most of the time. We cannot feasibly live in a perpetually transcendental state of oneness. However, it serves us well to be aware that infinity exists in any given moment and in any given direction.

Think about what you are doing at this very moment. For starters, you are reading this article in these pages of *The Witches' Companion*. That's an easy one! Now, consider how you are sitting, where you are sitting, and where you find yourself in time and space. Check! Next, bring to mind even more details about the present moment. Perhaps you are reading this on a bus. Or maybe under a tree, facing west. Or maybe under that same tree, facing east. There are many options and many possibilities, but in reality these potentials are endless and you could have chosen to alter any of these "realities" at any point in time.

Within the present moment, there is literally an infinite number of choices we can make. At this very moment, you might choose to move the pinkie of your right hand, or maybe the index finger. You might

choose to take a deeper breath than normal or maybe hold your breath for a split second. You might choose to look out the window for a moment, or you might glance to your left. You might choose to do any of these things at the same time right now, or maybe three seconds from now. Each of these choices is a "new reality" that you create;

we cannot go back and change even the smallest actions. Within life's *tabula rasa* (blank slate), you are writing the book of reality from moment to moment. Again, the possibilities we can choose in any given moment are literally endless; we can choose anything at any time. Life is like a "build your own adventure" book of monumental proportions.

It's overwhelming to realize that we can literally craft our reality at any time. Even seemingly inconsequential, everyday things are moments that we consciously dictate—and let's not even get into theories of the butterfly effect! It's also worth contemplating to what extent we craft our own reality versus the extent to which it is "prewritten" or predetermined. These deeper aspects of theology and existential philosophy are journeys we embrace as our metaphysical practices take shape, advance, and evolve on a personal level.

Spells, Rituals, and Healing Work in the Flow

Magickal work relies on the choices we make in any given moment. If we are connected to the present moment, aware of the nature of infinity, and feel at the top of our game, we can tap into the projective force of evolution propelling all energies forward in space and time. When we dance with life's progressive metaphysical flow, our magick and our art become crystal-clear; we know what to do and how to do it within our unique realm of knowledge and capability. From this space, we are riding the progressive wave of conscious evolution.

> **There's nothing wrong with research; it's essential to methodically craft our magick. However, the entire process of piecing together information and writing a spell or ritual becomes nearly effortless when we are in the flow.**

When there is magickal or spiritual work to accomplish, we can achieve a high level of success when we are in the flow.

We've all been there: poring laboriously through loads of books and websites to search for the right ingredients, incantations, or symbols to use for a spell. There's nothing wrong with research; it's essential to methodically craft our magick. However, the entire process of piecing together information and writing a spell or ritual becomes nearly effortless when we are in the flow. Rather than poring over research in frustration, our intuition will guide us to the resources we need. When we are in the flow, we will know which websites to click on and which symbols or words to use. When we are in the flow, we will know which herbs to add, subtract, or substitute during magickal work, and we will find that our intuition (and perhaps our spirit guides and guardians) easily communicates components and procedures of spells or rituals. When we are in the flow, we know what to do, where to look, and how to accomplish our magickal or creative goals, whether for ourselves or for others.

There are times when I will get a request for a healing spell or prayer but will not engage in the request until I have a moment of being in the flow. When this vibrational alignment occurs, the magick simply creates itself, because I am not preoccupied with stress over time, money, food, or any other sort of distraction. From this energetic flow, I intuitively know which herbs and stones to use for the sachet I'm crafting. I know which gods or spirits to work with for a particular issue. I know how to perform a ritual with confidence and clarity.

When aligned with the flow, we can more easily see the bigger picture of any given situation, and can be of much better assistance as a result. Whether it's Witchcraft, ceremonial magick, hands-on healing, prayer, meditation, or artistic work of any kind, everything makes sense and comes easily when we are in the flow with life's infinite dance.

Finally, for those who would like to study dharma and the yogic process of aligning oneself with life's greater purpose, I earnestly refer you to Kauai's Hindu Monastery, which is searchable on YouTube (try the video "What Is Dharma?" on Kauai's Hindu Monastery channel) as well as online at http://himalayanacademy.com. Here, one can also sign up for the monastery's daily lesson emails and download a plethora of free PDF books written by its illustrious founder, Satguru Sivaya Subramuniyaswami.

Sources and Further Reading

Bennett-Goleman, Tara. *Emotional Alchemy: How the Mind Can Heal the Heart*. New York: Harmony Books, 2001.

Dass, Ram. *Be Here Now*. San Cristobal, NM: Lama Foundation, 1971.

———. *The Only Dance There Is*. Garden City, NY: Anchor Press, 1974.

Digitalis, Raven. *Esoteric Empathy: A Magickal & Metaphysical Guide to Emotional Sensitivity*. Woodbury, MN: Llewellyn, 2016.

Farrar, Janet, and Stewart Farrar. *A Witches' Bible: The Complete Witches' Handbook*. Custer, WA: Phoenix Publishing, 1981.

Greer, John Michael. *The New Encyclopedia of the Occult*. St. Paul, MN: Llewellyn, 2003.

McNevin, Estha. *Opus Aima Obscuræ*. Tradition materials and lesson notes. Missoula, MT: 2003–present.

Starhawk. *The Spiral Dance: A Rebirth of the Ancient Religion of the Great Goddess*. San Francisco, CA: Harper & Row, 1979.

Subramuniya, Master. *Merging with Siva*. Kapa, HI: Himalayan Academy, 2003.

Tolle, Eckhart. *Stillness Speaks*. Novato, CA: New World Library, 2003.

Raven Digitalis (Missoula, MT) *is the author of* Esoteric Empathy, Shadow Magick Compendium, Planetary Spells & Rituals, *and* Goth Craft. *He is a Neopagan Priest and cofounder of an Eastern Hellenistic nonprofit multicultural temple called Opus Aima Obscuræ (OAO). Also trained in Eastern philosophies and Georgian Witchcraft, Raven has been an earth-based practitioner since 1999, a Priest since 2003, a Freemason since 2012, and an empath all his life. He holds a degree in anthropology from the University of Montana and is also a professional tarot reader, DJ, small-scale farmer, and animal rights advocate. Visit him at www.ravendigitalis.com, www.facebook.com/ravendigitalis, www.opusaimaobscurae.org, or www .facebook.com/opusaimaobscurae.*

Illustrator: Bri Hermanson

The Magical Manager

J. Variable x/ø

Between your job and your magical practice, do you feel like you're leading a double life? Working for a living takes up a disturbingly large chunk of the time allotted to actually *live*. It can be frustrating when it's time to go back to work before you're ready to switch roles... but why should you have to? If you're going to spend a third (or more) of your lifetime on the job, your workplace is an ideal setting to apply your magical skills. You don't have to pursue a career *in* magic to build a career *with* magic.

There are plenty of ways (subtle and otherwise) to inject magic into your professional life. Some of these ideas might not fly unless you're the boss and get to call the shots in your workplace or are lucky enough to work from home, but whether you're the CEO, a part-time intern, or somewhere on the middle rungs of the corporate ladder, making your job a little more mystical can increase your chances of having a successful career.

Magic: A Full-Time Job

Starting your own business or career track is a magical act: you're about to change reality for yourself and your future clients. Think about your current and past jobs, your overall career path, and what you really want to get out of the work you do. Answer the following questions

honestly, like you would when planning any type of spell: How do you feel about what you do for a living now? What's your real underlying intent? Will success bring contentment or discomfort?

You know the drill for planning an important ritual. You make sure your intent is clear, and you think carefully about the techniques and tools you'll use to achieve it. You do the work, and then you act in accordance.

See the parallels between career planning and spellwork? Put these basic magical principles into play as you plan your future in the mundane world.

One of the first things a business needs is a good logo, one that is quickly recognizable at a distance and easy for people to associate with the name of your company and the nature of your work. It conveys a lot of information in the simplest possible form. In other words, a logo is a magical sigil! So don't just throw some clip art next to a font and call it good. This is your business's custom bind rune. Put some thought into it.

> **A logo is a magical sigil! So don't just throw some clip art next to a font and call it good. This is your business's custom bind rune. Put some thought into it.**

Next, your business's motto becomes your mantra, the repeating chant that raises energy and directs it toward your goal. In spellcasting you probably wouldn't want to sing "service and quality" over and over—that's pretty vague, and you know how the universe appreciates specifics. Let your motto tell people why they should care about and support your work.

In spellwork we often recite longer poems, prayers, invocations, or stories. This part of the spell becomes your mission statement. Expound on your motto with compelling language—you want to summon customers as well as the blessings of your deities.

Scheduling by the Stars

Many of us plan our rituals by the seasons, the phases of the moon, and the movements of the planets. You might try adapting some of these astrological principles to your daily business activities.

If your astrology skills are rusty, there are plenty of good books and tutorials available online that will help you learn enough to get started. Just staying aware of the prevailing celestial currents can give you a big advantage. You don't have to spend a lot of money or time setting up charts either, as there are a variety of astrology websites that will produce any type of chart in seconds (my favorite site is www.astro.com).

Of the twelve segments (or "houses") in an astrology chart, three directly affect your business: the Second House rules wealth and financial assets, the Sixth House describes how you can best serve your community (local or global), and the Tenth House rules your career path and public reputation. The nature of the zodiac signs ruling these houses and any planets appearing therein will tell you a lot about your best path to success and the obstacles you'll encounter on the way.

Don't stop with your own natal chart. Draw up charts for your partners, employees (or employers), investors, customers, and competitors. This will give you a lot of extra insight into their talents and challenges.

There are additional types of charts that can provide you with more details than just the natal aspects. A *synastry* chart combines two natal charts, highlighting the best ways the two people can work together and the interpersonal challenges they might expect. *Progressed* charts show how the influences of the planets and houses in a natal chart change as a person gains experience and wisdom over time.

Don't forget that your business itself has a "birthday," too! Think of your corporation as an entity with a life path of its own. Its charts can reveal a lot of information that might not turn up in the charts of the people involved with it.

Your Weekly Planner

In some traditions, every day of the week is assigned to a particular planet and its corresponding energies. If this idea resonates with you, try arranging some of the more important tasks in your schedule according to this system.

Monday (Moon, subconscious, waxing/waning energy): Brainstorming sessions, cleaning old stuff out of storage, following up on hunches

Tuesday (Mars, conflict, action): Competition, starting new projects

Wednesday (Mercury, communication, education): Research, general meetings, interviews

Thursday (Jupiter, abundance, good luck): Launching ad campaigns, entering contests, taking calculated risks

Friday (Venus, compassion, gentleness, finances): Negotiations, investing, team-building activities—and, of course, office parties!

Saturday (Saturn, limitations, perseverance): Reviewing projections and refining long-term plans, studying obstacles

Sunday (Sun, success, logic, conscious mind): Praise and appreciation of achievements, feasibility studies

Chaos Magic

One needs organization in order to run an organization. The most experienced chaos mage knows better than to put the forces of chaos in charge of the business (though that doesn't mean they won't try anyway). However, Eris and her minions, those unpredictable bolts-from-the-blue, can be invaluable teammates. Don't let your calendar, your meeting schedules, or your oh-so-meticulous business plan render your career path so rigid that it snaps under the least little change. Welcome surprises, even challenging ones—*especially* challenging ones; there are opportunities buried in every problem. Be adaptable and ready to explore new possibilities. A large part of success in any endeavor is the ability to be aware of all the different paths that one can take to get there.

The Subconscious Team Leader

Sleeping is supposed to be a break from reality, like a mini-vacation to a higher plane (or at least a more relaxing one). To dream about work can leave us annoyed and disappointed, but since we spend so much mental energy there, the subconscious is going to have a lot to say about it. Were you bored in your dream? Anxious? Implementing some crazy new idea? Finding a hidden passage in the back of your shop? Pay attention, because "work" dreams are full of useful clues and signposts that will tell you how you're doing and what you should be watching for.

> To dream about work can leave us annoyed and disappointed, but since we spend so much mental energy there, the subconscious is going to have a lot to say about it. … Pay attention, because "work" dreams are full of useful clues and signposts that will tell you how you're doing and what you should be watching for.

Bring your work with you into your meditative practices, too. "Mental rehearsal" is a visualization exercise in which someone only *thinks* about performing an action, imagining each detail of the activity step by step. Studies have shown that this focused mental work can in fact create neural pathways as the brain memorizes the activity, and it does improve one's proficiency in the real world. Mental rehearsal works for just about everything, from playing an instrument to improving at sports to developing positive habits and ways of interacting with other people.

Magical Office Space

Some businesses are just fine with blatantly magical décor. You might have to tone it down a bit for others, and there are some places where it just isn't appropriate at all. Even still, there's always something you can do to add esoteric environmental components to your ongoing career spell.

- If you've got room for a potted plant or two, try growing a tiny herb garden at your desk. You can add these herbs to your lunches or tea to help deal with any type of energy you might encounter during the day.

- Instead of keeping a dish of candies at your desk, how about a bowl of crystals? Polished stones and magical rocks are relatively inexpensive (especially if you order them in bulk), and you'll have a constant supply of tiny powerhouses full of different kinds of energy. You'll also find that people can't help but run their fingers through them when they come to your desk. Go ahead, give them away. The nature of the stones to which your visitors are drawn can tell you what they're seeking or what they value, and you can use this information to nurture a more productive business relationship with them.

- Your computer and mobile devices are teeming with energy currents that you can apply to your magical goals without anyone being the wiser. Your screen's wallpaper is there behind everything you do, so incorporate sigils into the design, or use an image of your deity(ies), a photo of your physical altar, or a charged geometric pattern. Online print-to-order shops offer mouse pads, phone and tablet shells, and laptop cases that you can have made with your own custom magical designs.

- Dream boards (handmade collage displays) are powerful magical constructs that help you keep your energy pointed toward your goals. Invest in a large cork board and put it up where you and your employees can see it every day. Invite everyone to contribute (perhaps anonymously) to this collective dream board by including pictures and quotes about your business, visual illustrations of your mission statement, and what each employee hopes to be able to contribute. This can be a great way to keep everyone at work focused not just on the direction of the business but on their own important role in its success as well. Even if you have no employees, a dream board is still a great inspiration to keep visualizing your goals!

- Want to keep negativity out of your workplace? Smudging is great, though not always feasible, but you can also trap the negativity outside before it ever gets in the door. If you control the décor, you might repurpose a dreamcatcher (or craft something like it of your own) to ensnare the heavier currents before they cross your threshold. If you want to be really sneaky, paint a cleansing sigil on the underside of your welcome mat and see who might hesitate a bit before entering. If you're unable to make physical changes like this in your workplace, remember that everything has an aura, just like your own body. The same visualization and shielding techniques that you use for yourself can be adapted and applied to cleansing and protecting a building or a room.

. . . .

Every day is one small step in your long-term magical spell, and there's always something you can do to push life a little closer to your goal. Don't forget one of the last and most important steps in magic: acknowledging and appreciating success! Manifesting your dream career is an enormous magical work. It will probably take years before your efforts pay off. It's easy to get discouraged and distracted from the work, but there are plenty of little milestones along the way that show you're on the right track. Give thanks for these. Make sure those who are helping you know that you notice and appreciate them. The more people who share your vision and contribute their energy to your "circle," the more successful your spell will be.

J. Variable x/ø *spent many years working for other people in bland, soul-crushing cubicle farms, where she would cast secret magic spells every day to improve her employment situation. Now she runs her own small business, which is devoted to magic and art, so we can cast spells during meetings and decorate our office with as much weird stuff as we please. Success! Please visit us at www.reverend-variable.com.*

Illustrator: Rik Olson

Roadkill: A Pagan Perspective

Kerri Connor

One day I was scrolling through my Facebook feed when a status jumped out and caught my attention. It was posted by a person I knew to be Pagan who was absolutely livid because a deer had jumped out in front of her while she was driving. She hit the deer, killing it, and in the process her vehicle had been damaged. As I read through the comments, I found she fervently blamed and cursed the deer. Several of her Pagan friends joined in, insulting the animal. People called the animal a "pest" and a "nuisance," and one even stated it was "suicidal" and suggested it was mentally ill.

I was mortified.

This woman took *no* responsibility for the death of the animal and saw nothing wrong with her own actions, and when I pointed out that perhaps there was a lesson to learn, I was insulted as well. Within hours there were dozens of comments. Some said they were happy she was okay, but many focused on the deer and how terrible the animal's actions were. I was at a complete loss.

According to my beliefs, animals and nature are sacred. But, as I was finding in this particular conversation anyway, people shared my beliefs only to an extent—the similarities ended when an animal walked onto a roadway. Neither the original poster nor the commenters were interested in hearing an opposing point of view. While we often see this type of behavior in political conversations on Facebook, I was surprised to see the same type of attitude on a topic of this nature. Excuses were made as to why it was the deer's fault and not the fault of the woman who killed it. Out of the hundreds of comments being made, I appeared to be the only person who was concerned about the deer. Getting a bit fed up, I finally asked if this was really seen as the appropriate way for a Pagan to view roadkill, and I was told that not all her friends were Pagan—totally dismissing the behaviors of those who were, and not acknowledging her own behavior at all. At that point, I decided this topic clearly needed a larger audience than it was getting, and so here we are.

While it may be true that some types of Pagans don't revere Mother Earth and nature as strongly as others, for the most part Paganism and an endearing fondness for wildlife tend to go hand in hand. Even non-Pagans tend to take certain precautions when in areas known to have an abundance of wildlife. The woman who hit the deer was the first to admit that there were many deer where she lived and they would often run out in front of cars. Some people take this as a sign to slow down, especially when there are signs designating that it is an area where deer tend to cross. These signs are posted to warn people that animals may be present and to proceed with caution. And most people understand that humans have taken over many wide-open spaces where animals used to roam freely.

Humans have encroached upon these spaces, taking them away from the animals, not the other way around. Since we are the ones building roads and using them, shouldn't the responsibility to keep them safe for all fall on us as well? Do we really expect animals to learn to stop, look, and listen before crossing a humanmade road? Or do we need to make sure we are being vigilant enough to protect the lives of animals as well as our own? Often accidents involving deer don't just damage the animal. Cars can be destroyed as well, not to mention human lives. Even people who want to blame the animals should be able to realize that travel in areas rich in wildlife needs to be done *carefully*, even if only to protect the people inside the vehicle.

For myself and many Pagans, a deer is an incredibly sacred animal, as it is a symbol of the God himself (depending on the tradition you practice). To see comments stating it was "just a stupid animal" was heartbreaking, but it was also a wake-up call that not everyone practices the tenets of their faith in everyday life. If a deer is the symbol of the God to you only during rituals, and is an intrusive animal the rest of the time, I've got news for you—your practice is lacking consistency.

I, and many other Pagans, believe that when an animal puts itself right smack dab in front of you where it *must* be seen and acknowledged, it is doing so for a reason, and that reason is *not* because the animal is a nuisance or suicidal. It's trying to deliver a message, one that you have obviously been ignoring.

In his book *Celtic Totem Animals: Meet Your Animal Helpers on Your Own Shamanic Journey*, John Matthews tell us this:

> The deer thus represents travel to the Otherworld or the Faery Realm, shape changing (the perception of the world from different viewpoints), and the natural deerlike qualities of gracefulness, swiftness, and keen scent.

A recent article titled "10 Animals as Omens When They Cross Your Path" says a deer is a messenger for Artemis, and that

> *seeing a deer is a symbol that Heavens know what you're going through and that you should continue facing these problems with Grace, Purity and Dignity. Deer keep their heads up even when hunted. Be like the Deer. Stand up and face the problems without losing your inner beauty. Become a beautiful Warrior of Life.*

This animal that has leaped out into the road has a very powerful message to bring to you—a message that is so important, the animal has risked its life to try to get it to you. This is a huge wake-up call, not a nuisance. The very first message is, of course, to *slow down* and look around you. Maybe there is another area of your life where you are just plowing through and not paying attention to others or to things happening around the situation. Take off your blinders and really look around and see what you are missing.

Not too long after I came across this post on Facebook, I was driving home with my twenty-three-year-old son. We both saw a turtle in the opposite lane slowly making its way across the road. I turned at the next street—less than half a block away from the turtle—to go back to where the turtle was. My son and I had done this numerous times in the past. I would pull up and he would get out and carry the turtle across the street and then hop back in the car. This time, however, as we waited to pull back out onto the road, three cars passed us by, all headed toward the turtle. It was only a matter of seconds, but we were too late to save him. Not one of the drivers so much as tapped their brake lights, and by the time we got there the turtle had been killed and terribly mutilated. We both cried. There was simply no reason for it. The turtle was large enough to be seen and there was ample room to go around it. Had the cars hit the animal on purpose? Possibly, but I don't know for sure. I do know that it appeared the turtle had been hit by more than one set of tires.

It doesn't take a genius to figure out that if there is a turtle in your path, the message for you is a great big thunderous SLOW DOWN! Obviously this message isn't just about your driving either. Have you ever noticed that when you travel the same road every day, you stop seeing it? You stop noticing homes, businesses, places on the side of the road, etc., because you always see them. Your eyes and mind begin taking the scenery for granted, and it simply doesn't register anymore. You drive on autopilot and miss the forest for the trees. This happens to us in other areas of our lives as well. Are there people you don't see anymore? Do you take their presence, their feelings, their actions, for granted? Do you simply assume they will always be there for you in the future because they have always been there for you in the past? Are you ignoring aspects of your life, such as your job or your health? The turtle is here to tell you to look at those things you no longer notice and really see them.

Different animals have different meanings, and different parts of the world have different animals, so the animals you see when you're out driving are obviously going to be different depending on where you live. What isn't different, though, is that these animals should be protected, not killed. They should be listened to, not griped at. If you kill an animal, particularly if it damages your car, instead of being angry with it, you should *thank* the animal. It gave its life to get a point across to you, to teach you, to help you. Your job is to figure out what that message is.

If you find yourself in this situation, take some time to think about it. Swallow your pride and resist the instinct to put the blame on the animal. Research what the animal means. There are plenty of online resources, books, and animal-related oracle cards that can assist you in finding out what messages different animals bring. *Thank* the animal for giving its life to help you. If you can, dispose of the animal's remains in an honorable way. Don't just leave it in the road to rot. It deserves more respect than that. At the very least, provide the animal with a blessing, move it to the side of the road (safely), and call the associated roads department to let them know a pickup is needed.

There are people who carry a kit in their trunk just for this purpose. A small shovel, plastic bags, and gloves make it safer to move an animal off the road, and smaller animals can be bagged so you can transport them with you. (Some places may not allow the removal of roadkill except by authorities, so know your local laws.) If you can, it's better to bury or cremate the animal and give it back to Mother Earth. If you have no way to bury or cremate an animal, or you need to leave it next to the road for some other reason, offer the animal a blessing. Keep some lavender buds, rubbed sage, or your own type of blessed water (moon water, Florida water, or whatever you normally would use) in your kit. Sprinkle some herbs or spritz some blessed water onto the animal and give it a blessing.

There are plenty of online resources, books, and animal-related oracle cards that can assist you in finding out what messages different animals bring. *Thank* **the animal for giving its life to help you. If you can, dispose of the animal's remains in an honorable way. Don't just leave it in the road to rot. It deserves more respect than that.**

Some Pagans also have a special prayer or blessing they use when they see animals on the road that were killed by someone else. You may want to add one of these to your repertoire as well. It's hard to know if these animals hold a message for you or not. Generally

I would say that the message was meant for someone else. However, if you start seeing the same type of animal over and over again, look up its meaning! Get the message now. Don't force the animal to jump out in front of you to deliver it.

There is another way you may encounter a dead animal that is more upfront and in your face, and that is if you find the animal on your property or on the road in front of your house. Don't take this as a co-incidence. This animal died where it did for a reason. The message it is delivering is for you or for someone you live with. Again, dispose of the remains honorably and thank the animal for its sacrifice. (Again, depending on where you live, some dead animals should be reported to your local health department, especially if the death does not appear

to be trauma-related. Birds and bats may be infected with West Nile or rabies. Be sure to check with your local health department for information on testing and disposal.)

Remember, we are not the only sentient beings on this planet, and chances are we weren't the first either. We should treat animals with respect and honor. We need to protect our animal counterparts, care for them, listen to them, and, yes, even learn from them.

Blessing for Animals Who Have Delivered Us a Message

This blessing is for animals whose death you played a role in, or for those that were found in your yard or on the road in front of your home (when you know the message is for you).

Thank you, beloved (type of animal), for your sacrifice.
I honor you and respect you.
Your message has been received.

Blessing for Animals Who Have Delivered a Message to Others

This blessing is for animals that died sending a message to others.

Thank you, beloved (type of animal), for your sacrifice.
I honor you and respect you.
May your message be received.

Resources

The Alchemist. "10 Animals as Omens When They Cross Your Path."
Magical Recipes Online (June 24, 2017). www.magicalrecipesonline
.com/2017/06/animals-omens.html.

Matthews, John. *Celtic Totem Animals: Meet Your Animal Helpers on Your Own Shamanic Journey*. Boston, MA: Red Wheel Weiser, 2002.

Kerri Connor *has been practicing her craft for over thirty years and runs an eclectic family group called the Gathering Grove. She is a frequent contributor to Llewellyn annuals and the author of* Spells for Tough Times. *Kerri resides in northern Illinois.*

Illustrator: Jennifer Hewitson

Magical Self-Care

Nurture Your Body, Mind & Spirit

Relaxation for the Busy Witch

Elizabeth Barrette

Everyone needs to relax sometimes. Finding the time to do that can pose a challenge. Happily, there are some methods of relaxation that combine well with other activities. Magical techniques can also shorten the time required to relax and deepen the effectiveness of other methods. Let's take a look at some ways to soothe your mind and body.

Guided Meditation

Guided meditation involves listening to someone narrate an inner journey for you to follow. This can be done along with another task or by itself. People often use such recordings while performing long, repetitive tasks, such as shucking a pile of corn. It's also a great way to wind down before bed. If choosing a tape for active use, make sure it doesn't make you drowsy.

You can buy recordings of guided meditations or find free videos online. There are also transcripts that you can read to yourself and record for later use or have a friend read aloud for you. Many people use guided meditation in solitary or group rituals. It's good for spiritual occasions when you want participants to let go and travel deep, or as a way to unwind after more strenuous magical activities. This technique combines well with many others and thus is one of the basic building blocks in relaxation practice.

Progressive Relaxation

Another basic technique is progressive relaxation. To do this, you tense and release muscle groups until you have covered your whole body. Most people find it easier to tense and release than to relax tight muscles from their current condition. Guided meditation is helpful for people who tend to lose track during this exercise. If you do this at night in bed, it becomes a great way of soothing yourself to sleep. Doing it in a chair at work or while traveling can help prevent stiff muscles from remaining too long in the same position. It also relieves stress if you get worried and tense while waiting for something. If you like doing trancework, progressive relaxation is a reliable way of achieving an altered state of consciousness.

A typical sequence begins at your feet. Tense and release one foot and then the other. One at a time, do your calves, thighs, and buttocks. Then do each hand, your belly, forearms, upper arms, chest, neck, and head. Don't worry if you can't isolate muscle groups precisely. Just do the best you can. Good practice makes good progress.

Breath Exercises

Everyone breathes, but not everyone breathes in a calm and efficient manner. Inefficient breathing can make people feel dizzy or panicky, so improving your breath is an effective way to relax. It can be done anywhere and takes no extra time because you have to breathe anyway. *Pranayama* is a branch of yoga that focuses on breath exercises, so there are many choices within it, but you can find other types of breath exercises elsewhere as well.

Deep breathing is the basic method, described in various ways. At heart, it simply means breathing from your diaphragm instead of your chest, so the lungs can expand fully. Your belly should rise up during a deep breath. This gets plenty of oxygen into your blood. Slow, deep breaths relax the mind. This technique does require you to pause what you are doing, but five to ten deep breaths take only a minute or two. Use this technique to calm yourself before tackling a problem.

Ujjayi, or conqueror breath, entails inhaling through the nose and exhaling through the mouth, passing the air over the back of your mouth. This creates a soft hissing sound that focuses your attention. It helps ground you in your body and shut out distractions.

Kumbhaka, or breath retention, belongs to hatha pranayama. It involves holding your breath briefly after an inhale (*antara*) or an exhale (*bahya*). It is typically spaced between several normal breaths. Kumbhaka helps with hyperventilation by making sure you inhale or exhale all the way and do not pant rapidly.

Yoga

The Hindu practice of yoga includes many different branches. As already mentioned, pranayama covers breathing, and it combines well with other types of yoga that focus on different parts of the body. This discipline features bending and folding the body into various positions. Some are easy, while others are quite challenging. Most can be done with a little practice. Yoga loosens the body and frees the mind. It is also readily available. Most locales have yoga classes within a reasonable distance, and there are plenty of books and websites if you prefer to learn on your own.

Practice yoga as much as you have time for. Some people do it every day, and others once a week. While it's great if you can spare an hour for a full class, many sequences require only ten to fifteen minutes. There's a tradeoff between length and frequency: If you can do yoga every day, you don't necessarily need as much time for each session. If you do it only once a week, then try to schedule one to two hours for best effect.

Surya namaskar, or sun salutation, is one popular yoga routine consisting of several moves with an up-and-down orientation. It has several variations. Many people like to begin their day with a sun salutation because it's invigorating and doesn't take too long. It helps you start out with a relaxed yet alert mood instead of feeling anxious.

If you need help relaxing after a hard day, then try *yoga nidra*, or sleep yoga. Sometimes this includes a brief routine of poses before bed, but it doesn't have to. You can go right to *savasana*, or corpse pose, lying flat on your back. Move your attention slowly from one body part to another. You may combine this pose with progressive relaxation if you wish. Yoga nidra also includes meditation on the topic of peace and calm. Experts can learn how to drop into a deep sleep while remaining conscious. This is a great goal if you are interested in the mystical applications of sleep and dreams.

If you want to improve your magical practice, consider kundalini yoga. It combines techniques of body, mind, breath, and more in pursuit of spiritual energy. Think of yourself like a hose. When a hose is crimped, less water gets through; when it's open, more water gets through. If you are tense, less energy gets through; if you relax, the flow improves. Kundalini yoga boosts your flow by releasing tension and increasing focus.

Mudras

Mudras are yoga poses for your hands that influence the flow of energy through your body. Do them with either the right or the left hand, or both hands together. They can have a variety of mental, physical, and mystical effects. Some people experience effects almost immediately, so mudras can be done in just a few minutes; other people need more time to make them work. Unlike whole-body yoga, mudras are discreet and portable. You can do them anywhere, and usually nobody will notice. Like whole-body poses, mudras also come in basic, intermediate, and advanced forms. The simpler ones are the most subtle, while some of the advanced ones are pretty obvious. If you have time for a

If you have time for a yoga routine, by all means incorporate mudras into it. A big advantage of mudras is that you can do them along with some other activity. They are perfect for staying relaxed anytime you need to wait.

yoga routine, by all means incorporate mudras into it. A big advantage of mudras is that you can do them along with some other activity. They are perfect for staying relaxed anytime you need to wait.

My favorite is a sequence of four mudras that is sometimes used in combination with the Sa-Ta-Na-Ma mantra. For the *gyan* mudra, touch your thumb to your forefinger, leaving the other fingers open and relaxed. This grounds and calms you and improves concentration. For the *shuni* mudra, touch your thumb to your middle finger, leaving the other fingers open and relaxed. This raises awareness and encourages patience. For the *prithvi* mudra, touch your thumb to your ring finger, leaving the other fingers open and relaxed. This increases energy while creating a sense of stability and self-confidence. For the *buddhi* mudra, touch your thumb to your pinkie finger, leaving the other fingers open and relaxed. This enhances mental clarity and intuition. This mudra sequence is so simple that children can learn it as an early technique for self-soothing.

For an intermediate choice, the mudra for dispelling fear (*abhaya* mudra) uses both hands. Hold up your right hand with palm facing forward, arm bent by your side, as if saying "stop." Relax your left hand and point it downward, as if dropping something. This mudra appears in many Hindu and Buddhist statues.

For a more advanced option, try the *acceptance* mudra. Curl your forefinger until it touches the base of your thumb. Reach your thumb

toward your pinkie finger, touching the tip of your thumb to the side of your pinkie near the end. Leave the middle and ring fingers extended and relaxed. This mudra reduces negative emotions such as sadness or anger, helping you to overcome resistance to a situation and just go with the flow.

Chakra Balancing

The body's energy flows along pathways very similar to the nervous system, following approximately the same routes. It pools in energy centers called *chakras*, of which the largest and most famous appear along the spinal column in a rainbow of colors. These seven main chakras are *muladhara* (root chakra), *svadhisthana* (sacral chakra), *manipura* (navel chakra), *anahata* (heart chakra), *vishuddha* (throat chakra), *ajna* (third eye chakra), and *sahasrara* (crown chakra). As in any other body system, the chakras may have too much or too little energy, or drift out of alignment in other ways. Usually it's too much energy that leads to people feeling tense or wired.

To balance your chakras, first consider the overall stack to make sure they're in the right place. If the line is uneven, energy won't flow smoothly between the chakras. Next, concentrate on each individual chakra to ensure it has the right amount of energy. If the energy level is too low, add more; if it's too high, move some of that energy elsewhere. Finally, visualize energy flowing up from your root chakra, along the line and out through your crown chakra like a fountain, and then cascading around you to form your *aura*.

Balancing your chakras should leave you feeling refreshed and relaxed. If you have difficulty achieving this balance yourself, you can find someone else to do it for you. There are energy workers who do it all with mystical forces, but other practitioners use stone magic to facilitate the flow of energy by balancing each chakra with a different stone that matches its color and energy.

Massage Tools and Stress Toys

Many useful tools can aid in relaxation. These are often sold as massage tools or stress toys. While the fancy therapeutic versions can be expensive, you can often find more affordable versions at an office supply shop or toy store. Look for items that make you feel happy or serene when you see or touch them. Some people like the natural tone and silky feel of wood. Others enjoy the bright colors and bouncy texture of plastics. You can even find a few metal ones.

A foot massager is a thick rod with bumps or rings on it. You can put one underneath a desk to kick around and play with. It helps to soothe your mind and keep your feet from cramping up. Since it's under cover, few people will notice it.

Stress balls come in countless styles. They can be smooth or bumpy and range from firm to springy to squashy. The stronger your hands are, the firmer the material should be. Using a stress ball releases emotional tension so you can relax. It also does a fantastic job of exercising your hands to reduce the chance of muscle cramps or repetitive stress injuries. If you have a firm, bumpy one, it can double as a massage ball: put it in your chair and sit or lean on it to massage your legs or back.

Baoding balls, or Chinese meditation balls, come in various sizes and materials. They often are made of metal, with a chime device inside that makes pretty music while in motion. The idea is to put two or more balls in your hand and keep them moving. Like other types of exercise balls, they strengthen your hands and relieve physical strain, but with the added feature of relaxing sound.

Fidgets comprise a wide variety of office toys. These are things that bend, twist, or come apart so you can play with them while you think. They are good for your hand-eye coordination, but they are used primarily for achieving a relaxed yet alert state of mind. Fiddle jewelry also falls in this category, if you have a ring, bracelet, or necklace with moving parts meant for manipulation. Remember, we humans used to spend most of our time with our hands occupied; only in recent decades have we become idle enough for our fingers to get bored.

Stone Magic

Stone magic is a popular and discreet practice that uses common rocks or precious gems to achieve desired effects. Walk into any Pagan or

New Age store and you'll see tons of crystals, rocks, jewelry, and other doodads made for this field. Be aware that there's a certain knack to stone magic; some people are very responsive to it, while others feel little or no effect. Good stones for relaxation include blue wild horse jasper, eye agate, goldstone, kunzite, lace agate, larimar, onyx, rose quartz, smithsonite, and strombolite. Boji stones balance energy. Shiva-lingam stones bring enlightenment and inner peace.

Jewelry is one of the most subtle options for stone magic. People see it but don't realize it does anything. For maximum effect, wear magical stones against your skin. Prayer beads can be worn as a bracelet or necklace and used to count mantras or other prayers. A chakra pendant has a main crystal, usually clear quartz, with a rainbow row of others to represent the chakras. This helps the wearer stay calm and focused. Some people find that copper or magnetic jewelry aids with various complaints.

A worry stone is a flat oblong with a hollow on one side, to be rubbed with your thumb. These are often made from onyx, agate, or other soft stones. If you need a silent pocket fidget, this is an excellent choice.

A desk fountain can be filled with ordinary rocks or tumbled gemstones. The water makes a soothing sound and cleanses energy. You can also find pebbles engraved with words such as *magic, healing,* or *calm.*

Herbs and Oils

Plants can help you relax in many ways. Just keeping a few houseplants creates a more tranquil environment. Scents can be soothing or invigorating. Dried herbs may be used in cooking or tea. Oils may be placed in a diffuser or worn as a personal fragrance. Both herbs and essential oils can be used to make dream pillows.

Drinking tea is a marvelous way to calm down. Just holding a warm cup helps you unwind, or in summer, iced tea will cool you off. Chamomile, lemon balm, linden flower, and passionflower are a few popular herbs to soothe the nerves. *Adaptogens* are substances that aid the body in adjusting to stress. These include elderberry, ginseng, holy basil, licorice, and maca root. Several of these also make excellent candy.

Aromatherapy offers many essential oils for relaxation. Popular choices include amber, bergamot, chamomile, jasmine, lavender, sandalwood, and ylang-ylang. Blue chamomile is particularly noteworthy for soothing magical complaints, like when you practice too long and get a headache.

· · · · · · · · · · · · ·

As you can see, there are many tools and techniques for relaxation. Choose the ones that appeal to you. Test to see what works. You may find it helpful to make a "relaxation box" containing a selection of soothing items. Try to include one for each of your senses: vision, hearing, touch, smell, taste, and mystical energy. While your state of mind/body isn't always under your complete control, it remains under your influence. Manage it wisely.

Elizabeth Barrette *has been involved with the Pagan community for more than twenty-seven years. She served as managing editor of PanGaia for eight years and dean of studies at the Grey School of Wizardry for four years. She has written columns on beginning and intermediate Pagan practice, Pagan culture, and Pagan leadership. Her book* Composing Magic: How to Create Magical Spells, Rituals, Blessings, Chants, and Prayers *explains how to combine writing and spirituality. She lives in central Illinois, where she has done much networking with Pagans in her area, such as coffeehouse meetings and open sabbats. Her other public activities include Pagan picnics and science fiction conventions. She enjoys magical crafts, historical religions, and gardening for wildlife. Her other writing fields include speculative fiction, gender studies, and social and environmental issues. Visit her blog,* The Wordsmith's Forge *(http:// ysabetwordsmith.livejournal.com), or her website,* PenUltimate Produc-tions *(http://penultimateproductions.weebly.com). Her coven site, which includes extensive Pagan materials, is* Greenhaven Tradition *(http:// greenhaventradition.weebly.com).*

Illustrator: Bri Hermanson

Unlocking the Magical Power of Polarity

Melissa Tipton

If you've ever lit a black altar candle for the Goddess and a white candle for the God, you've tapped into the power of polarity. Working with this principle intentionally can supercharge your magical practice. Think of polarity as a giant universal battery: the interaction between the two poles generates tremendous energy—energy that can be channeled to fulfill specific functions, anything from casting a spell to finishing a work project. In a spiritual sense, this polarity can be thought of as the interaction between the Goddess and the God; it is their dance that powers all of creation.

In our magic and in our lives, we can activate our own creative power by consciously working with the interaction between polar opposites, but in order to do this we first must embrace the paradox: these separate energies are, ultimately, one. They are two sides of the same coin, and understanding both their differences *and* their similarities is key. For this, we'll look to the Hermetic creation story, which begins with the All, a pervasive universal consciousness that is everything. In this story, the All chooses to separate itself into two distinct energies: the One Mind and the One Thing. Both the One Mind and the One Thing are still the All, because *everything* is the All, but they simultaneously exist in separate forms. This is the paradox of separation and unity. When they are separate, the One Mind and the One Thing are in a unique position to interact with each other, because now there is an "other" to interact with, and it is through this interaction—this polarity—that the universe was created.

We each possess our own version of the One Mind and the One Thing, our own internal polarity battery, and this interaction creates the life that we experience. Thus, learning how to work with these opposing energies in their various forms helps us become master creators rather than feeling as if life is happening to us. Why is paradox key when it comes to mastering polarity? Well, when we forget that the opposites are truly one, we get caught up in black-or-white thinking, and we can see this in the world at large. Nations are pitted against each other, and communities get locked into us-versus-them thinking. And in our own lives, we get caught in seeing circumstances, other people, and even ourselves as either right or wrong.

In this state, we're unable to tap into the creative power of polarity because we're too busy trying to get rid of the opposition that we've labeled as bad or wrong, and by doing so we dismantle our polarity battery. We're essentially hacking off one end of the battery. But when we return to the paradox that the opposites are truly one, we reassemble this battery. Our reality expands, growing large enough to hold, for example, our own opinions and those that run completely contrary to them.

> **We each possess our own version of the One Mind and the One Thing, our own internal polarity battery, and this interaction creates the life that we experience. Thus, learning how to work with these opposing energies in their various forms helps us become master creators rather than feeling as if life is happening to us.**

We can expand to make space for things that feel safe and comfortable and things that feel foreign and triggering to us. We no longer need to get rid of the opposition in order to feel okay, because our sense of reality has expanded to make room for all positions along the spectrum.

Just as importantly, we are able to accept the opposition within ourselves. Instead of shoving into the subconscious whatever doesn't match our ideal self-image, we expand to make room for all of our parts. In order for our internal polarity battery to function, we need to accept our internal opposites: our rational mind *and* our intuition, our body/physical nature *and* our soul/spiritual nature, the parts we like about ourselves *and* the parts we don't. When we can't hold space for both poles and the gradient of possibility that lies between them, we short-circuit our power, and this can manifest as a loss of energy, an inability to follow through on our plans and projects, or a feeling of being disconnected from our soul's purpose.

Working with the Energy of Polarity

To return to a state of balance and ignite our inner polarity battery, we'll start with a simple energetic exercise. Rub your hands together vigorously for ten seconds. Pull them about six inches apart, palms facing, and slowly move your hands closer and then farther apart until you can sense the energy pushback between them. It might feel like electrified taffy, pulling slightly if you move your hands apart and offering a squishy resistance when you bring them closer together.

Let's expand this sense of polarity with a yoga pose: tree pose. Stand with both feet planted firmly on the ground, feet hip-width apart. Even in this standing pose, feel how your feet push into the earth and the earth pushes into your feet, creating a lifting effect, supporting you against the force of gravity. To move into tree pose, place the sole of one foot on the inside of the other leg, just above the ankle, on the shin, or on the inner thigh, whichever placement feels most

comfortable; just avoid placing your foot on the knee joint. In this pose it's common to wobble and sway, but let's use polarity and feel how this affects our balance. Rather than letting your standing foot rest passively on the earth, really press your sole into the earth, and feel how this lift travels up your standing leg and into your torso, giving your entire body more buoyancy.

Then work with the polarity between your lifted foot and your standing leg: press the sole of your lifted foot firmly into your standing leg, and just as firmly press your standing leg into your lifted foot. It's as if the leg and the foot are trying to push each other over, and so they each must push with equal intensity to avoid toppling. Feel how this opposition lifts your entire body, naturally engaging your core. Experiment with releasing the opposition to see if it's harder to maintain balance without it. This exercise gives us an embodied sense of the power of polarity. Rather than seeing opposition as a negative force that must be eradicated, these exercises allow us to experience its power. When we use polarity in tree pose, we can maintain our balance while exerting much less energy than we might if we were simply trying to stand up really straight without falling.

If you'd like to try a more advanced pose, move into dancer pose, or Lord of the Dance pose, which refers to Shiva, whose cosmic dance powers creation, a fitting analogy for our polarity work. Stand once more with both feet planted firmly on the earth, feeling the lift travel up both legs as you press the soles of your feet into the ground. Bend your right knee behind you and reach back with your right hand to grasp the *inner* edge of your right foot. It's common to reach for the outer, pinky-toe edge, but grasping the foot from the inside allows your chest and shoulder to open. Take a moment to bring your hips back into alignment if one side has dipped down or rotated forward or back. See if you can bring your knees in line under your hips, instead of allowing the bent knee to wander out to the side. Raise your left arm up to the sky, palm facing forward, bicep against your ear. Feel the energy traveling up and down the entire length of your body from foot to hand.

> **Rather than seeing opposition as a negative force that must be eradicated, these exercises allow us to experience its power. When we use polarity in tree pose, we can maintain our balance while exerting much less energy than we might if we were simply trying to stand up really straight without falling.**

Begin to press your right foot back into your right hand while you simultaneously resist this pressure by pulling forward against the kick with your right hand. You are using the polarity between the backward push of your foot and the forward pull of your hand to buoy you up. Stop here or continue by hinging at your hips, slowly shifting your torso horizontally as your left arm reaches forward. The key to balance is continuing the push-pull polarity between your right hand and right foot, even as you move. Add the polarity of pressing back in space with your lifted right leg as you simultaneously reach forward with your left arm. Experiment with releasing the dynamic push-pull of your right foot and hand and see if that makes it more challenging to balance. When you're ready, slowly come out of the pose.

These poses embody the power of polarity. Rather than trying to maintain balance through sheer force of will, clenching our muscles and holding our breath to stay upright, polarity generates a natural lifting force. The same is true in life: When we work consciously with opposition instead of trying to get rid of it, the energy it generates supports us; it lends power and flow to our actions, both magical and mundane, in a way that requires less forcing and clenching. Instead of depleting our energy stores by using sheer force of will to make things happen, we feel energized by allowing our polarity battery to do what it does best: generate energy.

When we work consciously with opposition instead of trying to get rid of it, the energy it generates supports us; it lends power and flow to our actions, both magical and mundane, in a way that requires less forcing and clenching.

Let's translate this to your magical practice, returning to the example of the black and white candles. Place these candles on your altar space, perhaps in the traditional orientation of Goddess (black) on the left and God (white) on the right. As you light each candle, imagine that you are switching on two poles of an immensely powerful battery. When both candles are lit, visualize the energy flowing between them, like the energy flow you experienced between your hands in the energy exercise and throughout your entire body in the yoga poses. Here are just a few ways to utilize this energy of polarity:

- If you are making a potion, tea, or other magical brew, place it between the two candles, visualizing the energy flowing into the mixture and imbuing it with power. If your brew is for a specific purpose, such as healing, use your intent to take the raw creative energy of polarity and channel it for healing. With the magical mixture between the two candles, place your hands on either side of it. Hold your intention for healing in your mind, and as the polarity energy flows from the candles, it passes through your hands, becoming imbued with your healing intention as it fills your magical brew.

- If you are feeling low-energy or out of balance, sit between a black and a white candle, allowing the energy to flow into you, activating your own internal balance of opposites and recharging your polarity battery. You might choose to meditate in this space, asking for guidance on how to use polarity more effectively in your magic and in your life. Or draw a tarot card, rune stone, or other divination tool in this space to receive guidance on mastering the art of polarity.

- Charge a piece of jewelry or a crystal between the two candles, and wear it to help you feel connected to your internal polarity battery. You can also use the following incantation, perhaps holding or focusing on the charged object as you recite it, anytime you feel low in energy or when you're experiencing conflict and are tempted to try to eradicate opposing forces:

Black and white,
Betwixt and between,
I embrace the unity unseen.
Hidden in the either/or
I make space for All,
My power is restored.

Using Polarity to Reduce Conflict

In our daily lives, there are many opportunities to tap into the power of polarity. One simple (yet often difficult!) practice is available whenever we find ourselves in conflict with someone. Perhaps their opinion differs from ours and we feel tempted to argue or try to persuade them to our way of thinking, or perhaps someone needs or wants something that feels at odds with what we need and want. It's common for our ego to start staking out its territory, digging in its heels and preparing to defend its position. We can relate this to the clenching and tightening sensation experienced in the yoga poses when we attempt to balance without using the energy of polarity to assist us.

We can shift our awareness to our Higher Self by pausing, taking some deep breaths, and finding our center. If this is hard to do in the presence of the "opposing" person, excuse yourself and go to the restroom to calm down and collect yourself. If you've charged a piece of jewelry using the method in the last section, now would be a good time to use it and the accompanying incantation to reconnect with the beneficial aspects of opposition. Your ego is convinced that you won't be safe unless it eradicates the supposed opposition, so another helpful measure is to reaffirm your safety. Feel your feet planted in the earth (or your body seated firmly in your chair), and feel the earth

rising up to support you. Allow this lifting sensation to travel up your legs, into your core, and all the way to the crown of your head, suffusing your entire being with a feeling of support and grounding. Repeat to yourself: "I am safe, I am safe, I am safe. All is well."

Bring to mind the image of the black Goddess candle and the white God candle, seeing the potent creative energy generated by their polarity. See how this opposition exists within your current situation. While it might be uncomfortable to experience disagreement or conflict, know that this opposition generates energy, energy that, in and of itself, is neither good nor bad—it's neutral—and how you choose to channel this energy will determine your experience of it. Recognize that your ability to see both poles of the opposition proves that you are bigger than either one: you are bigger than black or white, you are bigger than your opinions versus someone else's. You can expand and make space for both to coexist. In fact, your Higher

Self already exists in that plane of expanded reality—this is how you can see both poles. It is only the ego, with its limited viewpoint, that gets stuck in choosing sides.

Bring this expanded awareness back to the situation. Feel the oppositional energy within you, and know that you always have a choice in how you channel it. You can funnel it into the ego's us-versus-them agenda, or you can channel it into an expanded view of what is possible. A spectrum of options exists between the poles, and this spectrum encompasses ways for everyone involved to get what they need. The more you choose to identify with your Higher Self, the more visible these options will become, and the less attached you'll feel to defending your stance. A simple "I feel like there's a way for everyone to get what they need here. Can we brainstorm options?" opens the door. Your Higher Self leads with the knowledge that your perspective can coexist alongside differing points of view, and no one is damaged or compromised in the process; on the contrary, everyone's experience is enriched by the diversity, and powerfully creative energy is generated. Use this energy to weave your magic, and know that you always have access to this internal, infinitely renewing battery of polarity.

Melissa Tipton *is a licensed massage therapist, Reiki Master, and tarot reader who helps people hear and heed their soul's calling through her healing practice, Life Alchemy Massage Therapy. She writes extensively about witchy living and offers online classes and tarot readings through her websites, getmomassage.com and yogiwitch.com. The rest of her time is spent digging in the garden or hiking with her husband in the woods (aka looking for faeries).*

Illustrator: Kathleen Edwards

Chakra Spells

Tess Whitehurst

E ssentially, magic is energy work. It's sensing, shaping, shifting, and directing energy in order to manifest positive change. As such, a working understanding of the chakra system is an invaluable tool for magical mastery. Not only does it sensitize us to focal points in our body and energy fields related to various magical aims, but it also provides a highly accurate diagnostic tool to alert us to all manner of inner challenges and blocks, as well as the means to heal them, release them, and clear the way for divine flow.

A lifelong interaction with our chakra system harmonizes us with both earth and cosmic energies, grounds us, opens up our inspiration and intuition, relieves anxiety and overthinking, helps us communicate clearly and lovingly, helps us express our personal power and reach our goals, heals our sexuality, and facilitates a healthy balance of giving and receiving in all forms. It's truly a holistic form of magic: preventative, cumulative, and working on many levels at once.

As you may know, chakras are energy centers that lie along your spine. *Chakra* means "wheel" in Sanskrit, and the chakras are indeed like vibrational wheels of light. There are seven main chakras, each of which corresponds with a point in the body, a color of the rainbow, and other attributes related to mind, body, emotions, and life conditions.

Next, you'll find introductions to all seven chakras, as well as holistic magical work and effective spells corresponding with each. I suggest doing one or more of the holistic activities in tandem with any corresponding spell you choose to perform.

The Root Chakra

The root chakra is a ruby-red, horizontally spinning wheel of light at the base of your spine. When you sit on the ground or a chair with your spine straight, it's the part of your tailbone that feels the connection between your body and the earth or chair beneath you.

Just as the name indicates, this is the place where you root down into Mother Earth's energy and draw up magnetic, grounding light.

The root chakra's magical aims include feeling safe in the world, at home in your physical body, and supported in a healthy way by a loving community of family and/or friends. It's also related to trusting that you have all the tangible resources you need, now and always. Conversely, it's about letting go of what you don't need, particularly on the physical plane (i.e., stuff related to your body and belongings), but also negative, false, and disempowering stories about yourself.

Holistic Root Chakra Magic

Simply spending time in nature can help activate and balance your root chakra. So can walking barefoot or sitting on the earth, gardening, baking, cooking, hugging trees, and working with crystals and stones.

Root Chakra Spell for Feeling Safe in the World

This is a good spell to do if you have a general uneasiness or anxiety about your physical safety and well-being.

Ingredients
- Rooibos tea

- Boiling water

- Mug

- Optional: sweetener and milk of your choice

Brew a cup of rooibos tea (also known as red tea). Sit comfortably on the floor, using a cushion if necessary. Alternatively, sit in a chair with your feet flat on the floor and your spine straight in a comfortable way. Hold the mug in both hands, feeling comforted and grounded by its heat. Say:

I am a beloved divine child,
Cradled by my Mother the Earth,
Warmed by my Father the Sun,
Supported and nourished in all ways.

Mindfully drink the tea. Enjoy its earthy taste and feel its fortifying warmth. Feel it relaxing you and aligning you with an abiding sense that you are safe and all is well.

The Sacral Chakra

The sacral chakra is a bright tangerine-orange, vertically spinning wheel of light in your lower belly area. In women, it's the highly sensitive and emotional womb center.

This energy center is related to the water element and our sense of ease and flow, particularly with regard to the emotions, sexuality, senses, desires, and creativity.

The sacral chakra's magical aims include owning and expressing our sexuality, allowing and honoring our sensory desires (such as for food, relaxation, physical adornment, and sexual pleasure), loving and expressing reverence for our bodies, healing and strengthening the reproductive organs, and bringing both children and creative projects into the world.

Holistic Sacral Chakra Magic

Dancing while tuning in to your senses—particularly while moving your hips—will help balance and activate your sacral chakra. So will sending love to your lower belly through the palms of your hands. Mindfully enjoying sensual treats such as sex, strawberries, or soaking in a hot bath can also help bring this area into alignment.

Sacral Chakra Spell for Healing an Eating Disorder

Of course, it's important to treat eating disorders with professional counseling. This spell will help supplement your other efforts to heal.

Ingredients
- 1 or more bright orange candles
- The peels from 1 organic orange
- 4 drops essential oil of neroli

Draw a warm bath by the light of the orange candle(s). Add the orange peels and neroli oil. Before getting in, direct your palms toward the bath. Visualize it glowing and pulsating within a larger sphere of vibrant, blindingly bright tangerine-orange light. Say:

My mind is divine, my body is divine, my spirit is divine.
I invoke divine assistance now: may I love my body and treat it accordingly, with courtesy, reverence, and love.

Soak for 20–40 minutes, feeling your sacral chakra relax and harmonize with the bright orange energy you've infused into the bathwater.

The Solar Plexus Chakra

The solar plexus chakra is your own personal sun: it's a vertically spinning, yellow wheel of light at your upper belly area, above your belly button and below your sternum.

This area is associated with the fire element, and it's related to willpower, success, confidence, empowerment, physical energy, disciplined action, and the concrete manifestation of your goals.

This chakra is important for working successful magic because it synthesizes the energies associated with the physical world of matter and the infinite inspiration of the cosmos so that you can do what you intend and birth your fondest visions into tangible reality.

Holistic Solar Plexus Chakra Magic

To clear and activate this area, you can dance to rhythmic music, drum, run or hike, breathe consciously, clear clutter from your home, or laugh deeply. If there's something you've been putting off or have been planning to do for a while, finally taking action on it (even just a baby step) can also help get this chakra flowing.

Solar Plexus Spell for Busting Out of a Rut

This spell will help you get unstuck so you can take effective, joyful action on your goals.

You Will Need

- A square of yellow fabric

- 1 tablespoon coarsely ground Himalayan pink salt

- A yellow ribbon or cord

- A safety pin

Spread the fabric out in bright sunlight. Place the salt in the center of it. Sense the salt absorbing the purifying, bright-yellow/white light of the sun. Gather up the corners of the fabric, and use the ribbon or cord to tie it all up into a neat little bundle. Use the safety pin to attach the charm to the inside of your clothes so it's resting above your solar plexus. Set a timer for five minutes and spend the time breathing consciously while focusing your attention on your solar plexus area. Then unpin the charm and place it on your altar. The next day, repeat the five-minute breathing process with the charm pinned above your solar plexus. Continue daily until your energy is fiery and flowing.

The Heart Chakra

At the very center of your sternum is your heart chakra. You know exactly where it is because it's your emotional center. It's the place that aches with grief and swells with love. This is a vertically spinning wheel of vibrant, emerald-green light.

At the very center of your sternum is your heart chakra. You know exactly where it is because it's your emotional center.

Associated with the air element, this area relates—simply and profoundly—to love: giving love, receiving love, and being love. Just as "getting to the heart of an issue" means finding its core essence, our experience of this chakra is what makes us quintessentially human. The divine frequency is pure love after all, and the truth is, love is all there is. Everything else is an illusion. Magical aims of the heart chakra include love and relationship magic, deep emotional healing, and awakening to the preciousness of the moment and the beauty of everyday life.

Holistic Heart Chakra Magic

You can open and harmonize this area by crying deeply for any reason (even by watching a sad movie), listening to heartfelt music you love, breathing consciously, doing yoga regularly, being outdoors around healthy plants and trees, and mindfully appreciating your beloved animals and humans.

Heart Chakra Spell for Opening the Heart to Love

If you'd like to attract a new romance, but you can feel that your heart is currently closed to such energies, this spell will open you up and magnetize the love you seek.

Ingredient

- A green aventurine (crystal)

Cleanse the crystal by running it under cold water, holding it in bright sunlight, and/or bathing it in smoke from a bundle of dried white sage. Then sit comfortably, settle in, and clear your mind. Using your right hand, hold the crystal to your heart chakra area. Place your left hand over your right. Now bring your awareness to your breath. Simply notice as you breathe in and breathe out. When your breath naturally begins to get very deep and long, focus your awareness on your heart chakra and take four long, deep breaths, making sure to breathe all the way in and all the way out. As you breathe in, sense, imagine, and feel your heart chakra getting even more blinding in its brightness. As you exhale, see it spin more quickly while expanding to fill your entire chest. Say:

> *I am open to love. I invite love. I see everyone as lovable, including myself. I embrace every opportunity for love. I trust life and I trust love.*

Keep the crystal with you until your romance arrives.

The Throat Chakra

As you might guess, your throat chakra is located at your throat area and radiates throughout the entire neck region. You can envision it as a vertically spinning wheel of sky-blue light.

This area is associated with distilling what is true for you and articulating it through language, song, inflection, nonverbal sounds, symbol, action, art, and all other forms of communication. It also has to do with listening deeply to others and allowing for appropriate periods of silence and space between your words. Perhaps most essentially, this chakra is about aligning with your most authentic motives, so that you are truthful not only with others but also with yourself.

Magical intentions related to the throat chakra include speaking your truth, finding your voice, expressing yourself through art, and communicating clearly and effectively in all aspects of life.

HOLISTIC THROAT CHAKRA MAGIC

Chanting, singing, and vocal toning all help clear and activate the throat chakra. So does public speaking and finding the strength to say what's true for you at any given moment.

THROAT CHAKRA SPELL FOR FINDING YOUR VOICE

This spell will help you communicate with the world in a way that feels authentic to you, through an art, cause, and/or career path.

Ingredients

- 1 cup drinking water

- A light-blue drinking glass or water bottle

- 3 drops forget-me-not flower essence (the homeopathic remedy, *not* the scent)

Just before sunrise on the day of a full moon, pour the drinking water into the bottle or glass and add the forget-me-not flower essence. Just as the sun becomes visible above the horizon, hold the water in its light and say:

My true voice shall now arise,
Strong and clear, true and wise.

Drink the water, internalizing the sky blue of the glass and the flower as well as the fresh, bright energy of the rising sun. Visualize and sense your throat chakra glowing and spinning with vibrant, sky-blue light. Begin to chant *Om* over and over again, feeling the vibration of the sound further awakening your throat chakra and attuning it to the frequency of the Divine.

The Third Eye Chakra

In the middle of your forehead, about an inch above the center of your eyebrows, is your intuitive center: your third eye chakra. You can think of it as a quarter-sized, vertically spinning wheel of bright indigo light.

In the middle of your forehead, about an inch above the center of your eyebrows, is your intuitive center: your third eye chakra.

This energy center is the seat of your psychic awareness, intuitive knowing, and ability to see the underlying patterns at work in any given situation. It's also the place where you focus clearly on your intentions in order to manifest them: to bring them from inner vision into outer reality.

Obviously, this area is important for successful magical work because it allows us to mentally conjure up what it is we want to create, and to place our magical focus on it before it's actually present in the physical world. It's also related to magic for focus, concentration, and increasing psychic abilities.

Holistic Third Eye Chakra Magic

Any time you perform visualization exercises of any kind, you're simultaneously activating and awakening your third eye chakra. Other natural ways to energize the third eye chakra include performing tarot or oracle card readings, eating blueberries, and coloring, painting, or drawing with vibrant colors.

Third Eye Chakra Spell to Awaken Your Psychic Abilities

If you hope and suspect that you have psychic abilities, then you can be assured that you do. This spell will open the door to them.

Ingredient

- An indigo or royal-blue bindi (i.e., an adhesive skin ornament, available online and at Indian import stores)

Just before sunset, relax and center yourself. Just as the sun sinks below the horizon, affix the bindi to your third eye area. Begin to breathe consciously and feel as if you are breathing in and out of your third eye chakra. When you feel ready, say:

My third eye is open, and three visions I own:
That which is true, that which is hidden, and that which I am shown.

The Crown Chakra

Imagine a white or violet lotus blossom floating on the top of your head, like a freshly fragrant, flowering beanie. This is your crown chakra, the place where you receive energy and love from the Divine.

When this chakra is open and balanced, you are deeply aware of your true identity, which is infinite. Although there is the unmistakable appearance that you are a separate, finite human being, you know beyond a shadow of a doubt that the true reality is that you are eternal, vast, and one with everything.

Magical intentions related to the crown chakra include getting into divine flow, healing depression, awakening inspiration, and deepening your connection to Spirit.

HOLISTIC CROWN CHAKRA MAGIC

A regular meditation practice opens the crown chakra, as does heart-felt prayer, ecstatic dance, or spending time in quiet contemplation with flowers.

CROWN CHAKRA SPELL FOR DIVINE ORCHESTRATION

This spell will help you get into an easy and harmonious life flow, rather than experiencing life as one annoying hassle after another.

Ingredient

- Tea tree essential oil

Before bed, place a bottle of tea tree oil nearby. As soon as you awaken the next morning, lightly anoint the top of your head with the oil and say:

> Angels, pour light into me,
> Attune me to life's melody.
> I dwell in love and release my fears.
> I dance with the music of the spheres.

Feel, sense, and imagine a lotus of bright white and/or violet light blooming at the top of your head, harmonizing you with your most ideal life momentum and flow.

Tess Whitehurst *believes that life is magical. She's the founder and facilitator of the Good Vibe Tribe Online School of Magical Arts and the author of a number of books, including* Holistic Energy Magic, Magical Housekeeping, *and* The Magic of Trees. *Watch her videos, read her blog, and find lots of free resources to inspire your path at www.tesswhitehurst.com.*

Illustrator: Tim Foley

Self-Love and Magickal Power

Melanie Marquis

Self-love is essential to achieving our full potential in magick as well as in the everyday world. In theory, loving one's self is a very simple and straightforward thing to do, but in reality it often doesn't come quite so easily. Throughout our lifetimes we are told and taught by the outside world what we should think of ourselves, whether or not we matter, how valuable we are, and exactly what we deserve or don't deserve. Words and actions all leave their mark, and no matter how logical and sensible we may be otherwise, over time these seeds of self-doubt and self-loathing inevitably take

root. We begin to take to heart and act on beliefs that we know good and well are utter nonsense.

It's amazing the discrepancies and contrasts that can exist between how much and how easily we're able to love others and how poorly we may be inclined to treat ourselves. We may have no problem overlooking the faults and flaws of others, but if we ourselves make a slip, there can be a strong compulsion to punish and berate ourselves.

When we're unable to love ourselves like we love others, it creates a blockage that inhibits our ability to raise and project the energy required to fuel our magick. This is because magick travels along the threads that connect all things, and if we don't truly feel that we are just as valid and as valuable as the outside world, it's harder for us to harmonize with these energies and tap into them. This causes a disconnect in the mechanisms responsible for conducting the power that makes the magick possible.

You might envision it like an electrical circuit, with the energy and intention you're putting into the magick on one end of the circuit and the desired magickal outcome on the other end. Any doubt or disbelief in the energies or processes you are using for the magick, including doubting or disbelieving in yourself, creates a gap in the pathway along which your magick must move. This puts you at a magickal deficit right from the start. Magick can travel over such gaps if there is enough energy put into it, but if you're feeling fully connected with all that is, that gap won't be there in the first place and you'll find your spells much easier to cast and much more effective.

How can you possibly expect to cast a powerful spell if you're constantly telling yourself that you can't do anything right? How can you operate as the magickal and spiritual creature that you are if you feel about as worthy as a pile of poop? Self-loathing and magick just don't jibe. It's like a chef trying to make a good meal out of ingredients they find disgusting, or a mechanic who sets their tools on the hood of the car and expects the engine to fix itself without any of their own involvement. All the candles and herbs and ritual tools in the world can't make up for a lack of personal power, confidence, and ability. There is no way to take one's self out of the magick completely, and if your self isn't fully accessible due to insecurities or other forms of self-directed negativity, your magick doesn't stand a chance of working as well as it would otherwise. Self-love is essential!

Continuing to wear the hurts we've suffered has a heavy price. All our energy and strength turn inward to shield us from further harm. We become closed, small, defensive. While building a shield around yourself and suppressing your emotions can be a great survival skill to help you cope with moments of severe trauma, once these traumas have passed, it's much more effective, pleasant, and fair to yourself to liberate your inner power and allow it to radiate so brightly that the darkness itself shrinks from your presence. Reclaiming your power from the pains and sorrows and shields in which it is trapped is a wonderful way to be loving to yourself, even if it hurts initially to do so.

Digging down to the roots of long-held or deeply felt pains can be an ugly and difficult process, for sure. It is indeed a process, and it's a process that takes time, patience, and diligence. When we begin to really explore our feelings toward ourselves, old traumas and hurts that have long been suppressed have a way of rising up again, and it's only human nature to want to slam that book shut and take off running when this occurs. If you do run away, you'll only run right back to where you started, where you are right now, holding yourself back with doubts and insecurities that will water down and inhibit even the most powerful spells. Each of us has been allotted our own share of all that is, and it's a waste of all that goodness to do anything less than acknowledge and accept our magickal potential and utilize it to the maximum.

More important than a successful spell is a successful you! You deserve to feel good and happy. You deserve emotional healing. You deserve to love yourself! Be diligent and determined in your pursuit of self-love, and you will eventually and inevitably find your way back to your own heart. Try these rituals to help kick-start the process of embracing yourself with love.

> **More important than a successful spell is a successful you! You deserve to feel good and happy. You deserve emotional healing. You deserve to love yourself! Be diligent and determined in your pursuit of self-love, and you will eventually and inevitably find your way back to your own heart.**

The Mask in the Mirror Ritual

This ritual invites you to face, challenge, and strip away any negative, limiting, and inaccurate beliefs about yourself that are getting in the way of your ability to love yourself completely and without condition. Ugly, unpleasant, and hurtful feelings will be brought to the surface to begin the process of healing these pains, so be sure you're ready and that you have the time you need before you begin.

For this ritual you will need a large mirror (full-length or bathroom mirror–sized), a roll of masking tape, and a permanent marker.

Stand in front of the mirror and look at yourself. Let your feelings flow naturally, the negative ones as well as the positives.

Next, think about the hurtful labels others have placed on you. Consider also any unpleasant or unkind beliefs you have about yourself. Write a word or phrase or draw a symbol to represent each of these hurts on small pieces of the masking tape. Affix each piece of tape to the mirror so your reflection is partially covered by the tape.

Allow yourself to feel the effects that each word or phrase brings up within you. Let your emotions flow, and imagine that these hurtful emotions are being released from your body forever.

Next, close your eyes and take some deep breaths. Shake out your arms and legs to help clear your head. When you open your eyes, try to see yourself fairly and objectively, just as you would see someone else. Step out of your head and try to move beyond your identity and ego so that you can gain a higher perspective and a more accurate view of yourself.

Open your eyes when you're ready. Imagine that you're not looking at yourself but at someone else, a completely different person who just happens to look exactly like you. Look in the mirror and imagine that this person you see before you has come to you for help and understanding.

Take a fresh look at those labels this person you see in the mirror wears. Are they true? Are they fair? Are they beneficial in any way? Would you put any of these labels on anyone else in the world you even remotely care about? Is there any good reason to continue carrying these hurtful words? Tell the person you see in the mirror that it's okay to let go of these untrue labels forever.

Peel the tape off the mirror piece by piece as you affirm the falsity of each negative belief. Wad up the tape or rip it into small pieces, then throw it away. Now look at yourself in the mirror just as you are, without those ugly labels. What do you want to believe about this person whose reflection you see before you? Choose words or phrases to describe these positive beliefs, and write each one on a small piece of tape just as you did with the negative phrases. Say each word or phrase aloud and let the meaning of these words resonate within you. Even if you do not yet fully believe these positive things, allow yourself to say the words and be open to the energies that begin to flow within you. Place each piece of tape on the mirror to surround, but not cover, your image. Affirm that these are beliefs about yourself that you would like to cultivate, then give yourself a big smile to complete the ritual.

Leave the tape on the mirror for as long as you can so you will be reminded of your positive traits every time you look at your reflection. It can take some time, but eventually the truth of your affirmations will begin to sink in and you will find yourself increasingly able to see yourself in a more positive light. When you're ready to remove the tape from the mirror, consider affixing it to a piece of paper or an index card so you can keep it near you in your bag or pocket and read through it for a boost of positivity and encouragement whenever you need it.

The Nature of You Ritual

This ritual will help you open your heart to the idea of loving yourself unconditionally. Go outside to a place where you can enjoy the sights and sounds of nature. Sit quietly in observation until your mind is still and your heart is calm. Place your hands on the earth and feel the strong, stabilizing energy surge up from the ground and into your body. Look around and find something beautiful in the environment. It might be a tree, a rock, a mountain, a little bird, or whatever you see nearby that you admire the most. Does this small part of nature on which you are focused have to do anything to earn your affection, or do you love it simply because it is? And are you not just as worthy, just as valid? The truth of the matter is that love doesn't have to be deserved or earned. Love simply exists, and you can allow it to flow freely, restrict it, or block it out completely. Notice how easily

your love for nature flows, then think about the fact that you, too, are undeniably a part of nature, just as the rocks, birds, squirrels, trees, oceans, rivers, and mountains are.

One key to learning how to love yourself unconditionally is to become more aware of the unjust and illogical nature of self-loathing and self-denial. If you love nature and you are a part of nature, then by extension mustn't you love yourself? If you love animals, shouldn't you love yourself just as much as you would any other furry, scaly, or feathered friend? If you believe in human equality and in showing compassion, shouldn't you include yourself in that and give yourself the same care, respect, and consideration that you would offer to any other human?

If only for a moment, see yourself as a rock or a tree or a river, or see yourself as you would see any other human. Allow a feeling of love to flow freely from you as well as within you. Let this positive energy surround you and envelop you like a loving hug. When you're finished, look on the ground around you and select a small stone, twig, or other natural treasure. Carry this with you to help you remember that you are a valid and valuable part of nature that is deserving of love.

Melanie Marquis is the creator of the Modern Spellcaster's Tarot (illustrated by Scott Murphy) and the author of several books, including A Witch's World of Magick; The Witch's Bag of Tricks; Carl Llewellyn Weschcke: Pioneer and Publisher of Body, Mind & Spirit; Witchy Mama (with Emily A. Francis); Beltane; and Lughnasadh. The founder of United Witches Global Coven and a local coordinator for the Pagan Pride Project, she loves sharing magick with others and has presented workshops and rituals to audiences across the US. She lives in Denver, Colorado.

Illustrator: Rik Olson

Conjuring Confidence

Monica Crosson

It was March and it was wet. The rain had been falling nonstop for a week, saturating the ground until it could hold no more. It filled my shoes with muck and my heart with a damp dreariness, and once it set in… well, not even a triple shot caramel mocha with a healthy shot of vodka was going to pull me out of my March slump. So when I received a call from the Washington State University extension office asking me if I would prepare a PowerPoint presentation about a new gardening program I had been involved with for families experiencing food insecurity, my mood lightened. In fact, I felt good.

Why? Because of all the educators and master gardeners who had been involved with this program, they chose me to speak in front of our county commissioners and various other state and county officials about a proposed program to teach low-income families how to grow healthy food for their families, in part by buying seeds and plant starts with their food assistance vouchers. Yes! They chose me!

As I hustled about the house that afternoon, a million ideas popped into my head: the pictures I would use, the analogies to be made, what I would wear, and how I would speak. But in the far reaches of my mind, there was something troubling—whispers of inadequacy that I tried desperately to hush. So in an effort to take control of my confidence, I repeated: "I am a creative, intelligent person who is capable of great things." It worked—until I received another call later in the week.

"Thanks again," the master gardening program director said near the end of our conversation. "I am so pleased you have agreed to do this, Monica." She was pleasant and seemed genuinely happy about my involvement.

"Well, thank you. I'm excited to be a part of the project," I said.

"Oh, before I go, I forgot to tell you the presentation will be televised. I hope that doesn't bother you. It's only public access. I did hear they might use a clip for a short news story, so dress appropriately."

Oh, dear Goddess! "Not a problem," I lied. "I'm glad you told me, though, because I was considering wearing my pajamas," I said, making a lame attempt at a joke.

She laughed. "I'll see you in two weeks, Monica."

If my confidence had been wavering before, it took a full-blown nosedive after learning my presentation would be televised. It didn't matter if it was "only" going to shown on public access or if the chances of it being on a local news station were slight. I wished she'd kept that tidbit of information to herself, as it increased my stress level tenfold. I was convinced I couldn't do it. So what did I do? I did what any other mature, adult woman with a job and a family of her own would do: I went to see my mom.

"Oh, Monica. You always do a good job at whatever you do. Stop thinking poorly about yourself." The voice of my mother was soothing. "You're a very talented woman."

"Well, you kind of have to say that," I said with a weak laugh. "You're my mom."

She put her hands on her hips, just like she had done when I was a child and untruths had fallen from my lips.

"Come on, honey. If they didn't have confidence in your abilities, do you think they would have asked you to do it?"

I sighed. "No."

"Be proud of yourself. Everyone else is."

Later, my daughter, Chloe, who was ten years old at the time, came to me with a cloth bag she had made. Inside was a very large, unusual necklace. It was composed of thick red yarn strung with a mixture of large red wooden beads and very large blob-like beads she had made from polymer clay. Etched into the blobs were little winged dragons. I looked at her and smiled. "Thank you, sweetie."

"It's a bravery necklace," she said. "I made it and invoked the power of the dragon to help you find your confidence."

"I think this is just what I need," I said as she helped me tie the necklace around my neck.

The next two weeks ran relatively smoothly. I worked diligently on my presentation, enlisting my boys for help with the PowerPoint program. I memorized my speech, picked out a simple black dress, and prepared myself for possible questions. I meditated and repeated my mantra: "I am a creative, intelligent person who is capable of great things." I calmed my nerves with lemon balm and borage tea and tried to maintain a positive attitude. The night before my presentation, I called upon the Valkyries for a fierce spirit and a powerful boost of warrior-like determination.

The morning of the presentation I awoke feeling pretty good. There were no butterflies flitting about in the hollow of my stomach and I held down my breakfast (which was a plus). I met with some of the officials before the presentation, and they were easygoing and friendly. Why had I built this up to be such a monster? I was actually enjoying myself. My presentation was first and I felt great. I introduced myself and started the PowerPoint

program, which showed brightly on a large screen. But when I looked up, I found myself facing the blinking red eye of the camera that was taping the presentation. I swallowed and cleared my throat. *What am I talking about? Why am I here? What's my name?* All of these questions ran through my head in an instant. Then I held tight the necklace Chloe had made for me and remembered my inner dragon. *I am a creative, intelligent person who is capable of great things.* I swallowed again and continued without a glitch.

The Black Cloud of Self-Doubt

This story is just one of many that demonstrate a lifetime of needless self-doubt in both my mundane life and (as a new Witch) my magickal life. As a young girl, I was the student who knew all the answers to the questions but kept her hand resting in her lap. I was the young Witch who felt strongly connected to an herb or a stone when spellcasting but didn't use it because I didn't trust my intuition. And I am the adult who still sometimes questions whether she is good enough, smart enough, or creative enough.

We're all human, and inevitably at some point even the most confident individuals struggle with self-doubt. It's that little black cloud that rains insecurity down on us. But if not dealt with, that little cloud can turn into a storm that can lead us to abandon a project, leave a spell unfinished, or walk away from an exciting opportunity. Acknowledging our feelings of inadequacy is a great first step. It can help us identify where these feelings originate and analyze possible solutions. Ignoring our self-doubt or denying a lack of confidence does not make the feelings go away. In fact, it can just make things worse.

So whether you're a magickal practitioner struggling with self-doubt in your ritual or spell work or you're just trying to navigate self-assuredly through your mundane world, here are a few ways to conjure a little confidence.

Go Outside

People who spend a lot of time in nature tend to have a better sense of well-being, less anxiety, and improved memory, not to mention the vitamin D we absorb outside can help elevate our mood and increase focus and creativity.

Spend time in simple meditation in a shady area communing with the spirits that dwell within the landscape. Find a sunny spot on your balcony and use visualization techniques to see yourself as a fierce warrior ready to take on the world. Next time you walk along the beach, release your fears and anxieties into stones, and ritually throw them into the water.

Celebrate the Little Things

Did you just prepare an amazing incense blend that is going to be perfect for your next ritual? What about the amazing jam you made and gave out as gifts at Yule? These are a couple of examples of things you may have done and brushed off as nothing. For confidence building to work, you need to celebrate what makes you special. I'm not saying you should throw a party every time a spell goes right, but you can go ahead and pat yourself on the back.

One great way to celebrate the little things is by indulging in a bit of dark chocolate. And by the way, dark chocolate can increase magnesium levels, which is calming and increases confidence.

Stay Curious

Keep your mind active by asking questions and being observant. Being open to learning helps open new doors of possibility and gives us a better perspective on how we, and others, see the world. So get out there! Take that class on tarot, learn to make soap, or dare to finish that degree.

Step Out of Your Comfort Zone

For growth and change to occur, we must face what we fear. Stepping out of our comfort zone can be challenging but will leave us with a greater sense of accomplishment, which can help us gain more confidence in ourselves and leave us ready to take on more.

For growth and change to occur, we must face what we fear. Stepping out of our comfort zone can be challenging but will leave us with a greater sense of accomplishment, which can help us gain more confidence in ourselves and leave us ready to take on more.

Start by trying to do one thing per month that may be out of your comfort zone. Maybe you're the type of person who has many talents but is only comfortable working behind the scenes—conquer those fears by leading a ritual with your coven or circle. How about teaching a class on spellcraft or tarot? You don't have to start in a large classroom setting—start out with a few close friends in your living room. When you get a little more comfortable, set up a couple of classes at your local library, community center, or bookstore.

Are you the kind of person who never strays from a recipe? Test your knowledge by creating your very own incense or tea blends. Try unusual spice blends to add a magickal flair to your favorite recipes. Put the spellbook away and try some magick using only your intuition as your guide.

Stay Positive

Using positive self-talk can help us to be more resilient when facing stress or challenges in our lives. Staying positive broadens our perspective and leaves us open to new possibilities, whereas negative self-talk can narrow our thinking—we no longer see the big picture, but focus only on the negativity.

Imagine what negative self-talk does to your magick! If you're preparing for a spell and the entire time you're thinking I *don't know if this will work* or *What if I'm not powerful enough?* well, guess what? The spell won't work and you won't be powerful enough. Using positive visualization is especially important if you're going to work magick. As you gather your supplies for a spell or ritual, visualize the results of what you want to achieve coming to fruition.

Spend Time with People Who Hold You Up

How can you feel good about yourself if you're surrounded by downers? Don't let other people's pessimism and limiting beliefs transfer over to you. Spend time with confident friends who hold you up and support you. This is true for the magickal folk in your life as well. I had a coven mate who was very critical of everyone and took every opportunity to patronize us. "Hmm," he would say, with one ear in someone else's conversation. "Interesting. I don't know if I would have invoked Hekate for that spell. Very interesting choice." His tone and disapproving stare would always convey the feeling to whoever he was speaking with that they'd just failed potions class.

Don't Take Yourself Too Seriously

You know the old saying "Laughter is the best medicine"? Well, when it comes to confidence building, this is most certainly true.

So you mispronounced the name of the deity you were invoking on Beltane. The ritual continued on just fine, and come on, it was funny, right?

A more lighthearted perspective can make challenges less threatening and elevate the mood of everyone around you.

Have a Cuppa

There's nothing like a cup of tea to settle the nerves and release anxiety. To make the perfect cup of herbal tea, a good rule of thumb is to use a heaping teaspoon of dried herbs to every cup of water. To avoid bitter tea, keep the water just below boiling and steep for 8–10 minutes. Add honey, if needed, and enjoy.

Here are a few brews that may help increase your confidence level.

Lemon Balm (Melissa officinalis)

Known for its calming effects, this herb can reduce symptoms of anxiety disorders.

Peppermint (Mentha x piperita)

Menthol is the key to this herb's capabilities. Known to stimulate the mind and enhance your mood, peppermint may boost your concentration level. Give it a try.

Ginger (Zingiber officinale)

This plant may suppress cortisol levels in the body, enhancing your mood and calming stress.

Licorice Root (Glycyrrhiza glabra)

This root may reduce symptoms of adrenal fatigue (caused by chronic stress) and can be used to brighten the mood and calm stress.

Lavender (Lavandula officinalis)

This longtime garden favorite can be used to reduce stress, promote restful sleep, and improve the mood. The scent alone makes me happy!

St. John's Wort (Hypericum perforatum)

This longtime mood enhancer has been used for centuries to relieve anxiety, depression, and insomnia.

RED CLOVER (*TRIFOLIUM PRATENSE*)

This beauty, found growing in many yards, has been linked to raising dopamine levels in the brain, which increases motivation and elevates the mood.

Confidence Reflection Spell

Sometimes we need a little extra something to remind us that we are powerful beings capable of creating beauty and inspiring others. This little spell can help do the trick by allowing you to see yourself with new eyes. Remember, as with any spell, you are the most important component. Your positive energy is vital for this spell to work.

You Will Need

- A hand mirror

- A red tealight candle

- A sharp object for carving (such as a nail, heavy needle, or small knife)

- A piece of ginger root

Lay the mirror reflective side up on a table. Light the tealight and place it beside the mirror. Use your carving tool to carve whatever symbol, sigil, or rune symbolizes courage and confidence for you into the ginger root. As you do this, visualize yourself conquering whatever is causing your self-doubt. Place the ginger root on the mirror and gaze down into the mirror. Imagine the fiery power of the ginger root absorbing your insecurity and replacing it with self-assurance. As you do this, say:

I have the power to create. I have the power to inspire. I am a reflection of the power of three. Let my magick hold—so mote it be.

Let the tealight burn out safely on its own. Bury the ginger root in the compost or garden.

Love Yourself, Warts and All

Above all, the most important thing you can do to gain confidence is to accept and love yourself for who you are. Don't dwell on your mistakes, take time to play and relax, and be grateful for your beautiful, imperfect self. Remember, you are a unique expression of the Divine—there is no one else like you. Own your talents and celebrate your strengths. Live your life doing what feels right to *you*.

. . . .

I still have that bravery necklace my daughter made for me to increase my confidence. I wore it when I trained to be a whitewater guide and when I had to take a driver safety course when working at the post office. And now it's hanging from the bulletin board behind my computer, so as I write and self-doubt raises its ugly head, I just look up and I know: I am a creative, intelligent person who is capable of great things. And guess what? So are you.

Monica Crosson *is a Master Gardener who lives in the beautiful Pacific Northwest, happily digging in the dirt and tending her raspberries with her husband, three kids, two goats, two dogs, three cats, a dozen chickens, and Rosetta the donkey. She has been a practicing Witch for twenty years and is a member of Blue Moon Coven. Monica writes fiction for young adults and is the author of* Summer Sage. *Her latest book,* The Magickal Family, *was released by Llewellyn in October 2017.*

Illustrator: Jennifer Hewitson

Curing the Magickal Hangover

Charlynn Walls

It is the morning after ritual. You feel like you have been hit by a Mack truck. Your head is full of cobwebs and your mouth is like the Sahara. That is when you realize that you didn't complete the basic grounding during ritual because you got caught up in the moment. What could you have done to prevent the magickal hangover?

Magickal self-care is a topic that does not get a lot of time and attention. As someone who has been working with magick and energy for close to twenty years now, I wish I had known more about this area when I was just starting down my path.

When I was younger I threw myself into spell, rituals, and events with reckless abandon. It was not until I was already in the midst of an issue that I would stop to think about what I could have done to avoid or alleviate most of the problem. Now that I am older (and hopefully wiser!), I try to take better care of myself and avoid the magickal hangover that occurs from not dealing properly with excess energy. I also need to give myself time to deal with the issues that arise while transitioning back to a mundane existence after being immersed in a magickal atmosphere for an extended period.

Ritual Overload

One aspect that most magickal practitioners deal with is ritual overload. This can be due to an intense ritual experience. Usually a day or two after our ritual, my coven members will talk via phone or text to see how the ritual went. There have been times during this download process when we have found that we did not feel like ourselves. We would debrief and see where we had gone astray and then come up with a plan to avoid that in the future. The problem usually stemmed from altering our normal ritual procedures in circle due to guests or an unexpected occurrence.

An example of this is the time we had a particularly intense ritual at Samhain. Each quarter invoked a different deity, and the individuals in those quarters entered an altered state of consciousness. Their physical characteristics embodied the deity they were channeling. Their body posture changed, as did the timbre and cadence of their voice when they delivered messages to the group. I noticed that one of our member's eyes had dilated so much that the whites of her eyes were barely visible. In retrospect that made sense since she had invoked Anubis. When we were ready for the ritual to end, the deities were asked to depart. We also experienced some interesting phenomena where candles snuffed themselves out as the quarters were dismissed.

All seemed well at first, and we assumed (wrongly) that the deities had all departed. However, it became clear over the course of the next couple of days that Anubis had enjoyed his time with us and had decided to remain. We discovered, after talking at length, that when some of the members had released their quarter, they had said, "Stay if you will, go if you must." Apparently, Anubis thought this was merely a suggestion. So they had to go through a more deliberate and specific release of the deity. Once they did so, we no longer experienced any issues.

The intensity of this experience left my coven sister feeling completely out of sorts and exhausted. It was over a week before she felt more like herself again. If you perform a ritual that is out of your norm, it is crucial that you brainstorm all possible scenarios by yourself or with your group. You also need to be specific in your intent and wording to ensure that everyone experiences the desired outcome.

Grounding

Excess energy from ritual can also be a problem. Improperly grounding during or after ritual can produce an abundance of energy running through the individual. This is often connected to ritual where a substantial amount of energy has been raised. There have been quite a few times when I have found myself in a circle and the person facilitating the ritual just sent the energy out into the universe. This practice allows the energy to run amok. It is better if the energy is directed toward your goal and with intention. Energy is much like lightning: it will follow the path of least resistance, and it will travel through the body of the individual in the circle. So if it is not properly grounded, the individual can experience headaches, sleeplessness, nausea, or other negative health effects.

There are other ways one can experience an abundance of energy. I am particularly attuned to the phases of the moon, and if I am not careful, I get a shot of energy during the full moon that is like an adrenaline boost. During this time I must take extra care to make sure I am eating well and getting plenty of rest. I will also take a walk in the evenings to help burn off some of the excess energy generated during this time.

When grounding, I personally like to kick off my shoes prior to raising energy so that if energy becomes trapped in the circle, I can immediately ground it into the earth. By digging my toes into the loam, I have a connection with the earth, and what flows in also flows out.

Grounding after releasing energy is a good practice as well. There are many ways to ground, and I suggest trying a variety to find the way that works best for you. I like to sit on the ground and place my palms on the ground. This positioning brings me closer to the earth, and I feel more stable and connected to the pulse of the earth. I am then able to breathe in and pull up the excess energy into my solar plexus. Then, as I exhale, I push the energy through my arms, out of my palms, and into the ground. I also like to take a shower after ritual so the water can wash over me and I can visualize any excess energy flowing down with the water.

Grounding can be completed immediately following the raising of energy or after the circle has been released. If you are feeling anxious or jumpy, you may need to ground again, and that is okay. If you cannot ground out all the energy by yourself, ask someone to help you. During large events there usually will be people designated to help with this exact task.

When I help ground someone else, I like to make a physical connection with them. I hold their hands or place my hands on their face or back, depending on what is most comfortable for that individual. Then I draw their excess energy into my hands and up through my arms as I inhale. When I exhale, I push the energy down through my core and out through my feet into the earth. It usually takes 7–10 repetitions to completely rid the person of the excess energy. Then I make sure to reground myself.

After Special Events

As a Pagan, I have attended my fair share of events. These can be festivals or magickal retreats where you, as the magickal practitioner, are surrounded by others of like mind. There are opportunities to actively learn about magick or practice it. Multiple rituals are usually conducted over the span of the event. Such events can be very positive and powerfully life-changing.

The downside of attending events is that they end. When they do, we can feel a little lost trying to negotiate reentry into the mundane world. The first couple of days after an event are typically the worst. At a minimum, we are tired. It is also not uncommon to feel sad, emotional, or unable to concentrate or to have headaches or loss of appetite.

The good news is that we were not the only ones who attended the event. If you are having issues readjusting to "normal" life, reach out to a friend. Talk about the experiences you had at the event. Social media makes connecting with others easier than ever.

When I was just a young Witchling, I attended a Mabon festival with a group of friends. We were a close-knit group, and there were some very intense rituals that weekend. Ritual started at dusk so we could walk to the ritual area. We could see the flickering of torches in the distance, and we were challenged along the way. The circle had already been established, and we had to cross the threshold. When we were permitted to enter the circle, I remember hearing it begin to sprinkle. However, once we crossed the boundary, not one of us became wet!

When you have a profoundly powerful experience, you want to experience that same intensity again. So the prospect of leaving and not having that opportunity again can produce anxiety. I began to have issues as I was packing up my tent. I did not want to leave, and it was a gut-punch to pull up those tent stakes and know that I had to go home. Monday was not an easy day at work. I was exhausted because I did not rest at the event—I was having too much fun!

At work, I was easily distracted and caught myself daydreaming more than once. I am typically very logic-minded, but I found that I was unusually emotional. Fortunately, processing with my friends who had attended the event with me was cathartic. I was able to honor the event and was feeling like myself again in a couple of days.

Top Ten Tips to Avoid the Magickal Hangover

Here are my tips to avoid a magickal hangover! I hope these serve you well.

1. Be well rested.

2. Plan ahead! Be specific about your intent and desired outcomes.

3. Release and direct energy to a specific goal or outcome.

4. Ground during ritual.

5. Take a break and rest if needed.

6. Eat! It helps you ground. You can do this during ritual with cakes and ale. Just make sure it is a combination of protein and carbs so the effects are longer lasting.

7. Ground again after ritual if you are feeling jumpy or anxious.

8. After an event or ritual, be proactive and check on coven members and friends to see how they are doing with the transition.

9. Talk about the experience and debrief together.

10. Be kind to yourself.

. . . .

Self-care is not something that many magickal practitioners actively think about. However, it is something we all should consider and incorporate into our practice. We need to be proactive and work to take care of ourselves.

As we work with and direct energy, we need to know how and when to ground. We need to find a technique that works for us consistently. If you have trouble grounding, that is okay. We all do from time to time. Ask someone you respect and trust to help you find a technique that works for you. Also, do not be afraid to ask someone to help you ground yourself.

We should also be kind and gentle with ourselves as we transition from an intense and immersive experience back to the mundane world. We need to take the time to rest, eat well, and prepare for our rituals and events. We need to give ourselves time to work through the emotions of the experience. Honor your feelings, process them with friends, and know that more experiences are to come. If you can accomplish these things, then you are well on your way to being successful in the rituals and events you undertake.

Charlynn Walls *is the CEO/president of Correllian Education Ministries, which oversees Witch School. A practitioner of the Craft for over twenty years, she currently resides in central Missouri with her family. She continues to share her knowledge by teaching at local festivals and producing articles for publication with Llewellyn.*

Illustrator: Tim Foley

Witchy Living

DAY-BY-DAY WITCHCRAFT

Witching on the Cheap

Ash W. Everell

Witchcraft is a fun, fulfilling, spiritual, but frequently expensive craft that, more often than not, ends up costing some serious coin if you—like me!—lust after every single pentacle candleholder and Himalayan salt lamp you come across. Luckily, witches have existed for centuries without the ubiquitous Pagan shoppe or occult Etsy store, so let's turn back the clock and examine some old, modern, and folk tricks to craft witchery on the cheap!

There are a ton of ritual tools, spell supplies, and other magical objects that

can be crafted, scavenged, repurposed, or gathered from nature and that work just as well—if not better!—than expensive tools.

Tools

Crafting, finding, or repurposing your own tools is just as effective, and perhaps even more personal, than buying a set of premade ones. You can customize and select your witching tools to perfection, and even create a more comprehensive aesthetic and powerful energy for your altar supplies and witching utensils than with store-bought supplies.

Wand

The best wands, I think, are just wooden rods that speak to you on a personal level (and trust me, I'm a huge fan of the gorgeous, bespoke, hand-turned wands you can buy). Go outside and find a length of wood with the thickness, pliability, and feel that you like, try to determine the type of tree it fell from, and consecrate it as needed.

You'll find the best way to build a rapport with your wand is by going out and feeling it out. If a branch doesn't grab you, try something different that does, such as a long candle for a Witch with a fiery affinity or a wooden spoon for a Kitchen Witch.

You'll find the best way to build a rapport with your wand is by going out and feeling it out. If a branch doesn't grab you, try something different that does, such as a long candle for a Witch with a fiery affinity or a wooden spoon for a Kitchen Witch. If you're absolutely after that luxe wand look, try using a simple penknife to shave or whittle down your stick or branch according to its natural shape. You can even rub beeswax on it to seal it and protect its fibers from mildew and moisture. (Hint: Rub from handle to tip to encourage the flow of magic.)

Altar Cloth and Altar

For an altar cloth, pick out a cloth napkin, a tablecloth, or even a scarf or shawl in a color you feel is powerful. Crates turned on their sides or boxes (avoid cardboard, since you might want to use candles in the future) make great bases for altars, and you can even keep all your witching supplies inside them. If you're in a pinch or don't have the necessary supplies, a viable option is to find a stable object of the right height (like a chair) and place a tray on it to create a surface.

Athame/Ritual Knife

For cutting herbs, directing power, or in ritual, many Witches have need of an athame, boline, or ritual knife. A plain table knife or butter knife may be used, and the handle can even be wrapped in string or twine in a color corresponding to your tool (black if you're making a "100 percent accurate Wiccan" athame, for instance, or white for a loose Green Witch interpretation of a working knife).

Cauldron

Trust me on this one: use a mug. Find a heatproof mug or perhaps an oil warmer that you like. You'll be able to use it to mix potions, seep herbs, and create incense mixes, among other things. As for finding a cauldron that can withstand heat, for boiling tinctures or burning herbs, you'll want to find a fire-safe container—that is, cast iron, certain metal pots, or stone—that you can consecrate as a magical tool. The obvious choice here is a pot or pan that you don't use anymore. Try to avoid surfaces that will break under high heat, such as glass or porcelain. If you've got an oil warmer, you can use the space for oil as a traditional (albeit tiny) cauldron working space, heated by the candle below.

Book of Shadows

Keeping a record of your practice is a super-helpful tradition. A Book of Shadows need not be fancy, and having a plain notebook or even looseleaf paper is all you need to start. Later on you can copy the pages into your "fancier" Book of Shadows, if you wish.

Bell

Find two objects in your house that go *ding!* without breaking or causing chip damage—that's it! I discovered that simply by clanging my pestle and cauldron lid together, I can make the most beautiful, resonant sound that is perfect for my craft. Try different noises (with care—never use china or glass!) with different "instruments" to find your tone. If you're not one to literally bang pots and pans together, you can use your own hands: clapping firmly and commandingly can easily take the place of a bell.

CANDLEHOLDERS

The best (and almost free!) candleholders I've found are old bottles. Wine bottles are perfect for taper candles, and for the freecycling-minded Witch, twin beer bottles make perfectly acceptable altar candleholders (you can even swap them out for seasonal brews as per the Wheel of the Year). For tealights, empty jam and Mason jars make great candleholders, as do glass tumblers and cups, wine glasses, and

other glass containers. You can create more formal candleholders by layering some sand or rocks as a base for your tealights.

As for the tiniest of spell candles—the classic four-inch chime— you can employ a bit of physics and ingenuity to prop it up. Filling a container with sand or rocks, then placing the candle in it so that it's supported upright, is a tried-and-true method for holding those candles that don't seem to fit anywhere.

Spell Supplies

Here are some inexpensive options for spell supplies.

Herbs

Check around your kitchen or garden for herbs, spices, and ingredients to use in green magic. You've probably heard this tip before, but your kitchen and neighborhood are great places to find herbs of the earth. Take the time to look up which wild plants and weeds are native to your region, and check to see if there are any to collect in your own yard. Common plants native to North America that can be found in the New England region, for instance, include cinquefoil, hemlock, dandelion, and Queen Anne's lace, all of which can be used for common folk remedies (excluding hemlock, which is poisonous and suitable mostly for sachets and careful binding or shadow work).

All-Purpose Oil

For candle dressing, spellwork, and anointing, use consecrated olive oil as an all-purpose oil. You can pour out a measure each time you need it, and bless it to your specific intent. If you're crafting specific oils for a purpose and don't have a traditional base oil, like almond or jojoba, use a more affordable option, such as olive or vegetable oil. Vegetable and canola oils are fine for topical applications, such as glamours or ointments, but should be avoided as candle dressing, as they are extremely flammable.

Specific Oils

If you don't have any essential oils to work with, you can infuse your bottle of all-purpose oil according to your personal preference by adding corresponding herbs and spices and then straining. To do this, you've got two options:

French Press

If you have a French press coffee machine, you can fill it with a base oil and then add herbs, flowers, and spices corresponding to your intent. After letting them seep for twenty-four hours to a week in a cool, dark place, such as a cupboard, you can press down the mixture using the French press and pour the resulting clear oil into a separate container to save for later use.

Coffee Filters

You can infuse your own oils with virtually no equipment by adding herbs to a well-sealed bottle of base oil. Use a glass container, and ensure it's clean. Try to leave as little air as possible in the container. Once sealed, place it in a cool, dark place for at least a week, ideally for a month or two. When it's done, pour the oil through a coffee filter—(Slowly! It'll take a while to drain!)—and into a new container to save.

Bottles

For spell jars, oils, and other crafts and practical storage, collect pickle jars, syrup bottles, free-sample perfume bottles, or anything else that comes in a glass vessel with a removable lid. These come in handy to use as spell containers, candleholders, and other miscellanea. Just be sure to rinse them out with a little salt and water first.

Practical Craft: Recycling Old Candles

If you're like me, your house/apartment/room/studio is a maelstrom of melted wax and leftover candle bits. You probably haven't thrown out the wax yet, in hopes it won't be a waste. Well, it won't! For now I share my time-honored technique of melting down old, half-burned candles into one new, perfectly earth-friendly altar candle.

1. *Gather your wax bits.* That's any wax drippings, melted candles, or half-burned or otherwise useless candles. You can separate them by similar colors, if you wish, but I find that most left-over candles turn a shade of pink or pearl (and the color will change as we go along, anyway).

2. *Take a heatproof bowl and a large pot.* The bowl should fit in the pot and be able to contain all your melted wax. Fill the pot with a small amount of water, maybe two inches high, to make a double boiler. Heat the water to a gentle simmer, then drop the bits of wax into the bowl. Stir until the wax is fully melted. Sprinkle a very small amount of salt in it to purify the wax of its old energies.

3. *Herbally infuse.* If you have herbs corresponding to your altar, or even general herbs of cleansing and security (such as rosemary, oak, or sage), drop them into your liquid wax. Stir them in, releasing their energies, and let simmer for a few minutes to infuse.

4. *Add oils and scents.* Turn the heat off and let the water stop boiling. While the wax is still liquid, add a couple drops of your chosen essential oil. (My altar oil is a rose/juniper/sandalwood blend, but yours can differ.) Stir to incorporate.

5. *Get your jar.* This will house your candle. Take a piece of wicking, which can be bought online or at a craft store or can be made by

taking very porous string and saturating it very well in melted wax, then leaving it to dry. Tie the wicking to a stick or pencil, then lay the stick or pencil over the jar so the wick hits the bottom. You can (and I do prefer this!) also drop in a corresponding crystal or stone, thus giving your candle a magickal base.

6. *Pour!* Now pour your melted wax into the candle! Wait a minute until the wax has cooled a bit so that you avoid "cratering"— when your wick sinks down into a hole. Make sure to leave a small lip so the flame is protected when it lights. Let the jar candle cool off somewhere safe, like in a sink or tub. When the wax has hardened, you can seal the magic with a knotted cord.

You can, of course, change the recipe to make candles of any type, not just general altar candles. I find that recycled jar candles end up burning for extraordinarily long periods of time.

. . . .

The key to witching on the cheap is creativity. With a bit of resourcefulness and an eye for seeing objects outside of the box, any Witch can have the supply cabinet of their dreams!

Ash W. Everell *is a Green Witch, writer, and illustrator who loves gardening almost as much as collecting punk vinyl records. They live in Los Angeles with their partner and an unruly kitten named Artemis and run the Witching blog* Theory of Magick *(http://theoryofmagick.tumblr.com).*

Illustrator: Kathleen Edwards

Fold In the Magic

Lexa Olick

Folding is often overlooked as merely a chore, but it can actually symbolize our nurturing energy, strength of spirit, and hidden power. Our hands allow us to unfold our creativity and turn simple daily routines into an art form. I think folding is a valuable art form because it doesn't require any artistic ability to experience its benefits.

My friends and family members all have their own little tricks to make housework more bearable, and that usually includes watching TV or listening to music. However, I've found others, like my late grandmother, who enjoy the act of folding on its own. In the case of my grandmother, folding laundry wasn't just housework for her; it was a way for her to express the pride she felt in caring for her home and family. Even when the housework piles up, I, too, find it relaxing to sit in the quiet and fold. I believe I have my grandmother to thank for that.

The drawers and closets of my grandmother's house were always sweet-smelling. When it came to housework, she did more than just fold the laundry. She would tuck herbs from her garden between the folds of the towels and clothes not only to freshen the drawers but also to promote luck and good health for her family. There was something very comfortable and safe about unfolding towels in my grandmother's home. Unfolding the towels was almost like unwrapping a gift. First there was the quick waft of fragrance and then a small bundle or sachet would fall from the folds and onto the floor. It was one of many small tokens of her love.

Those hidden treasures inside folds were my grandmother's unspoken reminder that she was always looking out for us. Her favorite herbs were chamomile and lavender, so a soft, heavenly scent always clung to our clothing. That scent would follow us throughout the day and remind us of our grandmother's presence in our lives and that her family was folded in the protection of unconditional love. We continued to find those little "gifts" for some time after she passed.

Folding invokes images of a parent putting aside a tidy pile of clothing for their child, so it comes as no surprise that folding is a symbol of nurturing and loving care. We often tell our families that we love them, but *how* we say it, such as through our actions, is just as important as *what* we say. It's often the little things that show how much we love someone. So even if we dread the task of folding a never-ending pile of laundry, we still care enough to do it for our family.

From time to time my grandmother would get overwhelmed with work, but she never let the boredom of household tasks or the agony of negative thoughts bring her down. Every time she folded those heavenly herbs into the clothing, she would regain control and let the day's tension melt away.

My grandmother led by example, so I also grew up to find folding relaxing. The art of paper folding was especially helpful because I could do it anywhere. It even helped me out of a bind in college.

My grandmother led by example, so I also grew up to find folding relaxing. The art of paper folding was especially helpful because I could do it anywhere.

In my final year of college, I took an education course that required me to work beside a teacher in her classroom until I was ready to teach a single, forty-five minute class by myself as a final project. Since I was also working on a degree in art at the time, I knew already that I wanted to teach an art lesson. I decided to do a presentation on the color wheel, because my childhood art classes had skipped over the basic foundations of art, which was always disappointing to me because I was a creative child.

I shared my lesson plan with a friend who was in the same education class. She loved that I had centered my lesson around a personal story. She decided that she, too, wanted to tackle a subject that was close to her. I didn't learn what that subject was until the day of our final project. She offered to present first, which I mistook as a kind gesture since public speaking used to give me the jitters. However, my jaw fell to the floor when I saw her pull out a color wheel. I knew I would have to think fast.

I had exactly forty-five minutes, and no supplies, to mentally draft a new final project that would include visuals and student participation. The pressure was on! I was so panicked that I could not focus. I started to fidget. I began to move my fingers like I was playing an invisible piano. It was like my hands wanted to grab something and bend it. That's when I thought of paper folding. Lined loose-leaf paper is abundant in classrooms, so I decided to improvise an art lesson around origami.

To my surprise, paper folding had a positive effect on the students. They perked up at the idea that the plain piece of paper before them had the potential to become anything. They actively participated in the class while I folded paper to ease my anxiety. I taught others to appreciate the art of folding just as my grandmother had taught me. It was really rewarding passing along to others a skill that could possibly bring them some relief.

Folded Pendant Tutorial

Folding is an action that provides a distraction and leads to focused attention. The repetitive movement can soothe our emotional distress and distract our minds from the tensions of the day. It shifts our focus to the folds. We concentrate on each crease and pleat so that the finished product is accompanied by a sense of accomplishment.

This project uses an accordion fold, which has a lot of repetitive movement. You can make this pendant whenever you need a distraction. The pendant itself can be made on the go, and then you can bring it home with you to place on a string.

This project uses simple supplies. The pendant is very boho-chic and uses the same supplies you would find in a scrapbook: paper, yarn, and a button. When making this project, I recommend thinking of an aspect of your life that you would like to see grow. A few examples are love, happiness, career, education, friendship, understanding, or health. If you pick a theme for your pendant, you can choose your supplies accordingly. For example, you might use pink or red paper to stimulate more love in your life.

SUPPLIES

- Scrapbook paper

- Scissors

- Stapler

- Yarn

- A wooden bead

- A button (the size of a dime or smaller)

- Craft glue

- Floss (optional)

Step One

Cut out a small but long rectangle from your scrapbook paper. The rectangle should measure 2 inches by 9½ inches. Most papers are okay for this project, but stay away from thick paper like cardstock. Feel free to draw a pattern or write a special message on the paper, but don't glue anything on it, like rhinestones, glitter, or ribbon. Those embellishments will make it difficult to fold.

Step Two

Lay the paper vertically with pattern side down. Fold about ⅝th inch up from the bottom. A quick way to measure ⅝th inch is to line up the fold using your stapler. The fold should be approximately the width of a staple. Flip the paper over horizontally so that the pattern side now faces you. Fold about ⅝th inch up from the bottom again. Repeat until all the paper is folded. It will look like an accordion when you're done.

Step Three

Hold the folded paper tightly together. Feed it into the stapler vertically and staple the paper right in the center.

Step Four

Fan out the folds, forming a circle. Fasten the ends on the right side together with a staple. Place your yarn at the center where the original staple is. Fan out the folds until it forms a circle again. Fasten the left side together with a staple, taking care not to staple the yarn.

When you fan out the folds, the paper grows and symbolizes life's endless possibilities. Each fold is a deliberate act and represents the thought and care you put into the pendant. When you fan out the folds, the pendant blossoms and encourages success. This type of fold promotes a long life for its wearer. The folds expand and spread until the ends meet and make a perfect circle. The image of the circle represents wholeness and gives us a sense of protection and safety as we embark on a new path in life that will hopefully allow us to meet with success, just as the folds meet to form the circle.

Step Five

Take both ends of the yarn and thread them through a wooden bead. Pull the bead down until it reaches the folded paper. The bead holds the pendant in place and keeps it facing forward so it can hang flat around your neck.

Step Six

Hold both ends of the yarn and tie them together with an overhand knot. Trim any excess yarn.

Step Seven

On the front of the pendant, glue a button at the center. Then set it aside to dry. You could also thread the button with floss and tie it to the pendant. All you have to do is thread the floss between the folds where the staples are. I recommend using a button that is the size of a dime or smaller. Anything larger than a dime would hide too much of the pendant.

Lexa Olick *is the author of* Witchy Crafts: 60 Enchanted Projects for the Creative Witch. *She has previously contributed to Llewellyn's other almanacs, such as the* 2018 Witches' Companion, 2015 Sabbats Almanac, *and* 2013 Herbal Almanac. *She is a graduate of the University of Buffalo, where she studied art and art history. Her artistic journey began as a web designer, but her true passions lie in jewelry design and doll making. When she is not writing or crafting, she spends her free time traveling, gardening, and adding to her collection of antique glassware. She currently lives in New York with her family and several hyperactive pets.*

Illustrator: Bri Hermanson

Using Pop-Culture Magick in Your Daily Practice

Emily Carlin

A great way to improve your magickal skills is to create a daily practice. Doing so can deepen your magickal connections, heighten your skills, and help you in your everyday life. Using pop-culture magick in these daily practices allows the practitioner to take actions as simple as reading a favorite book or listening to a favorite song and turn them into powerful and effective magicks. While the possibilities for daily pop-culture magick practices are virtually endless, in this article we'll go over two of the most natural: a morning centering practice and an evening protection practice.

Pop-culture magick (PCM) is any form of magick that uses an element of pop culture (books, movies, TV shows, comics, music, etc.) in its magickal mechanism. How that manifests and to what extent varies from practitioner to practitioner. It might mean calling on the energy of Dr. House for a healing spell, doing a guided meditation to speak to Galadriel about working with the energies of nature, calling on Jack Harkness for working on self-acceptance, or crafting a whole system of magick based on a particular world or fandom. The possibilities are limited only by your own imagination.

PCM allows practitioners to enhance their practices through energetic efficiency and emotional resonance. People get very involved with their fandoms (Doctor Who, Marvel, Game of Thrones, etc.) and invest huge amounts of energy into favorite characters and stories. The common actions of watching and rewatching your favorite TV shows and movies, adorning your house with merchandise, wearing fandom T-shirts, reading and writing fanfiction, etc., are all things that forge a connection between you and your favorite characters in largely the same way a practitioner would work to forge a relationship with a spirit, a faery, or even a deity. It's only logical to take advantage of that kind of energetic investment and use it magickally.

A great way to begin or strengthen a pop-culture practice is with a set daily practice. A daily practice is any magickal/spiritual practice or set of practices that you perform every day. These practices are used both to heighten spiritual connections (e.g., prayer or meditation) and to keep magickal abilities honed (e.g., reading tarot or simple candle spells). While daily practice is tremendously valuable, many practitioners see it as the magickal equivalent of calisthenics: something you know you should do but for which you rarely have the time or energy. PCM, by its very nature of drawing from a source to which you already dedicate a lot of energy, both makes a daily practice more natural to actually perform regularly and boosts its efficacy. Most people have some fandom or favored bit of media that they enjoy on a regular basis, be it through surfing the web, talking to other fans, enjoying and re-enjoying the original media, etc. It takes very little extra action to make those interactions intentional and meaningful beyond simple consumption. Linking your daily practice to something you already enjoy and look forward to doing makes it effortless. It also takes advantage of both well-worn paths in your mind and existing energy wells, making it easier for your energy and intent to flow to their target.

While there are extensive variations on daily practices, some of the easiest to begin with are simple morning and evening practices. Most of us already have some routine we've worked out to begin our day and some routine for going to bed at night. That often involves checking our email and social networks or some level of media consumption. Instead of adding a new step to your routine, see if something you're already doing can be made intentional. This could be looking at fandom images on Tumblr or Instagram, watching snippets of a favorite show, humming the theme from your favorite movie in the shower, reading

a passage from a favorite book before bed, and so on. Find where pop culture already has a place in your routine and make that magickal.

Once you've found your morning pop-culture moment, you can turn it into a deliberate centering practice. Taking a few moments when you first get up to think about what you want from your day and consciously aligning your energetic self with those goals can help you achieve them more easily and fully, all while strengthening your ability to move and manipulate energy. A fun and rewarding way to do this is to think of a pop-culture character you love who embodies the characteristics you wish to bring out in yourself. If you want to do well in difficult conversations, you might think of Pepper Potts or Atticus Finch. If you want to feel strong and capable, you might think of Luke Cage or Letty Ortiz. If you want to do well in academic pursuits, you might think of Hermione Granger or Willow Rosenberg. Then make your pop-culture moment involve that character, and consciously invoke the traits of theirs that you want to guide your day.

For example, if I know that my day will require persistence, determination, and the uncompromising pursuit of a goal, I might want to work with Inigo Montoya. I could draw on his traits by reciting quotes of his in my head while putting on my clothes or by rewatching scenes from The Princess Bride on my phone while waiting for the bus, all while allowing his energy to infuse me. Due to my strong connections with this film, very little "formal" magickal action is required for me to connect to its energies. All I have to do is think the words "Hello, my name is Inigo Montoya" and my mind is instantly transported to that scene and flooded with the energies of that character. By taking advantage of previous energy spent and connections forged with favorite characters, PCM takes much of the drudgery out of a daily practice.

These same pop-culture moments and relationships with pop-culture characters can be used to create a superb evening protection practice. One of the most effective and complex forms of traditional sleep-protection magick is the creation of a guardian thoughtform. Through PCM, a practitioner can greatly simplify this bit of advanced magick by calling on pop-culture characters that already exist in an energetic form almost identical to that of a well-made thoughtform. Further, pop culture is utterly saturated with warriors, protectors, and guardians, from Superman to Kung Fu Panda.

Pick your favorite defender and call on them to watch over you and your loved ones while you sleep. This can be done by humming the hero's theme music as you get ready for bed, reciting a catchphrase, or drawing their logo in the air while calling on them for protection. If your protector is popular enough, you may even be able to get a T-shirt or pajamas with them on it, so you can literally wear your defender like armor. I've been known to run Iron Man or Captain America movies as I fall asleep as strong protection magick. Choose a guardian character that resonates with you and makes you feel safe; they will watch over you.

Daily practices that incorporate pop-culture magick are easy, fun, and effective ways to enhance your magick. By easily fitting into our existing routines, PCM daily practices are much less onerous than more traditional practices, making it much more likely that we will actually do them. Further, they take advantage of the vast stores of energy we already pour into the media we love and use them to create efficient and effortless magick. The next time you sit down to watch your daily YouTube videos or reread a beloved book, think of the ways they might be used in a daily practice and make magick happen.

Emily Carlin is a Witch, writer, teacher, mediator, and ritual presenter based in Seattle. She currently teaches one-on-one online and at in-person events on the West Coast. For more information and links to her blogs, go to http://about.me/ecarlin.

Illustrator: Jennifer Hewitson

The Power of Color for Magic and Healing

Peg Aloi

Quick, without thinking, what's your favorite color? Most people have one, and it can be a clue to your personality. Red might mean you're passionate or full of energy; orange means you're friendly and sociable; green could mean you're calm or a lover of nature; purple means you're dramatic or maybe interested in unusual hobbies. The meaning of color can be tied to many different emotions and aspects of personality, and can be interpreted in subtle ways for every person. The particular shade or hue of the color matters, too. Think of the different feelings and thoughts evoked when considering navy blue versus pale blue, for example: the former is regal and serious while the latter invokes youth and innocence.

Many magical practitioners and healers use color in their work. The choice of color for use in magical workings is often based on a combination of personal preference, folklore, research, and intuition. Pink or red for love, green for money, white for protection... Why do we use these specific colors? The ceremonial and occult traditions that inform Wicca and other contemporary magical practices utilize systems of symbolic correspondences, including color symbolism, that can be useful for many purposes, from spellwork to healing to creating a specific effect within an environment. The vibrational power of color—that is, the effect it has on our physical being and psyche because of the subtle vibrations and energies it produces when we look at it—has been widely researched and its effectiveness well documented; and, of course, the ancients knew all about it, too! (Crowley covers it extensively in his book 777, based on his study of the Qabala.)

This article explores some of the inherent qualities of color and suggests diverse ways to use them in personal magical practice and healing modalities for improved physical, emotional, and mental well-being, magical focus, and attainment of goals. You need not be a magical practitioner or healer to use color to improve your life.

Magical Uses of Color

There's a reason why your favorite store, whether it sells clothing, books, or smartphones, arranges objects to draw attention to their colors. Human beings respond very strongly to color: it's in our history, and centuries of art, fashion, and imagery can attest to our fascination with it. Most occult or magic shops offer an array of colorful tools and materials to help practitioners. You can get a range of colors for candles, candleholders, robes, gems, altar cloths, and other items.

The system of correspondences used in contemporary magical paths is both complex and accessible, and color is one aspect of it. Elements, planets, gems, plants, animals, and perfumes are just a few things that can be employed when creating magical workings. In the Western occult tradition, which forms the basis of contemporary magical practices

within Wicca and other paths, many of these correspondences are interrelated.

Astrology has color correspondences for planets and signs, for example, and tarot decks, depending upon their artwork, use color to impart meaning and evoke emotional associations. Take Libra: ruled by the planet Venus, the goddess of love and beauty, this sign's colors are pink, pale green, and light blue. These colors are soft, feminine, and calming and are associated with love, beauty, youth, and innocence. Pink is the traditional color of femininity, romance, and love. Pale green implies springtime, youth, growth, balance, and renewal. Light blue is a color of optimism, integrity, and innocence and has a calming effect. Think of the way these colors are used in art, movies, and advertising: What sorts of images and associations come to mind? Would utilizing certain colors help remind you of pleasant or desirable associations and thereby strengthen your magical work?

Pink is the traditional color of femininity, romance, and love. Pale green implies springtime, youth, growth, balance, and renewal. Light blue is a color of optimism, integrity, and innocence and has a calming effect.

It's true that much of the "magic" associated with different colors arises from the emotional feelings and thoughts we tend to associate with them. Architects and designers use color to encourage certain emotional reactions in spaces. Blues and greens have been proven to have a calming effect, but, perhaps surprisingly, hot pink (also known as "drunk tank pink") has also been shown to help reduce stress and anxiety. Some of the magical correspondences of colors depend on subtle variations in hue.

For the most part, using bright colors is considered most effective for magical work because their vibration is strongest, but paler or more subdued shades might be good choices for certain situations. Green, for example, can have a number of different connotations. Bright green, what we call "kelly green" (think Saint Patrick's Day), is a pure shade of green useful for magical purposes that call for green's most potent association: money (or prosperity). But green is also the color of growth and fertility, so maybe a deep, rich shade of forest green would be more appropriate for workings having to do with creating abundance or getting pregnant or developing a "fertile" network of job contacts, for example. Pale green might represent the energy of spring, new beginnings, or planting "seeds" for development. Blue-green, aqua, or teal can be used for strengthening magical work connected to the water element—associated with music, creativity, healing, the throat chakra, and the realm of the emotions. Yellow-green hues (from spring green to olive) conjure up natural settings, the greens of nature, so these colors might be nice to encourage a garden project or initiate a healthy new diet with plenty of fresh green foods and produce.

The ways you can use color in magical work are limited only by your own creativity. Some people like to meditate on a color, possibly finding that, as time passes, other variations of the color become prominent (for example, your focus on yellow may yield to gold). Some people prefer to have a very concrete, practical approach to color magic, using color directly to deliver impact. Painting the walls of a room can have a constant effect, so be sure you want to have that color's energies in your life over the long term. This is especially important in rooms where we spend a lot of time, like the bedroom. Pale blue in the bedroom can be conducive to sleep, and warm red tones (from salmon to pink to burgundy) are meant to help encourage sex and affection. Neutral tones (grays, beiges, etc.) can be calming but also a bit "blah." Bright, electric colors are not recommended for the bedroom because

they can disrupt sleep. Pale purples tend to be soothing and may inspire visionary dreams. Deep purple has occult associations and is associated with Neptune (the planet of mysticism and dreams).

If you don't want to paint the walls, bringing color into your surroundings with fabric (drapes, wall hangings, pillows, throws, and artwork) is an easier and more flexible way to do it. You could even display favorite items of clothing in certain colors to reinforce your purpose. The rose-colored velvet hat hanging by the door could remind you to be open to love every time you leave the house, and that plaid scarf might strengthen your resolve to plan a trip to Scotland and find creative ways to help fund your travel. And, of course, wearing certain colors keeps you aware of that color's energy all day and night. You needn't dress from head to toe in green to work prosperity magic, but a well-placed scarf can help enhance whatever work you are doing toward that goal. You can choose jewelry with colored gemstones to lend a visually subtle but powerful element of color magic. Speaking of green, it is also a very healing color, and there are a number of ways to use color for healing.

Healing with Color

One of the most common ways of healing with color is to become aware of a color's vibration and focus on its properties for your purpose. You can use colored light in several ways. You could get a colored bulb for a lamp or put a sheer colored piece of fabric over a lamp shade and then visualize the colored light on yourself or an object. Wearing a particular color over a body part in need of healing is also a common technique. For example, if you have a sore throat, you could tie around your neck a scarf in a color healing to the throat chakra, like blue or green. In general, pink and white are colors used for healing, white because of its appearance of cleanliness, purity, and "cleaning the slate" and pink because it is the color of healthy tissue. Green is also considered a healing color because of its connection to new growth, health, evergreen plants, etc.

Some healers use correspondences drawn from systems like the *doctrine of signatures*, which identifies healing properties of plants based on the plant's similarities to body parts or organs; this is connected to the plants' associations with planetary rulerships. Flowers and fruits ruled by the planet Venus (like roses and raspberries) are known to be beneficial to women's health, helping tone the reproductive organs, for example. Using this same principle, you might place a vase of pink roses on your healing altar to help soothe menstrual troubles (but drink your raspberry leaf and rosehip tea also!), or you might wear a red shirt to help heal heart problems, a blue shirt for the lungs, or a yellow one for the liver. You can also utilize planetary color correspondences as they relate to certain body parts or ailments (red for Mars, black for Saturn, white for the Moon, etc.).

. . . .

The use of color for magic and healing is a vast topic, one only touched upon in this short essay. I encourage you to look more deeply into this fascinating area of magical correspondences. Once you begin to utilize color in more intentional ways, you will notice how much it affects your life on a daily basis: your moods and your general sense of well-being. Being able to find new meaning in our surroundings and make connections to our desires and goals through color can add a vibrant and pleasing dimension to anyone's magical path. Learning to heal with color also aids us in understanding our connection to the cosmos and the natural world.

Peg Aloi *is a media studies scholar, writer, singer, and professional gardener. She was the media coordinator for* The Witches' Voice *from 1997 through 2008. Her blog,* The Witching Hour (*www.patheos.com /blogs/themediawitches*), *focuses on Paganism and media. She is currently writing a book on the portrayal of witches in film and television.*

Illustrator: Tim Foley

Introduction to Glamour Magic

Deborah Castellano

What is glamour? Let's take a look at some definitions from Merriam-Webster:

glamour
glam·our noun ('gla-mər)

1. an exciting and often illusory and romantic attractiveness • the *glamour* of Hollywood; *especially*: alluring or fascinating attraction—often used attributively • *glamour* stocky • *glamour* girls • whooping cranes and ... other *glamour* birds—R. T. Peterson

2. : a magic spell • the girls appeared to be under a *glamour*
—Llewelyn Powys

Origin of *glamour*: Scots glamour, alteration of English grammar;
from the popular association of erudition with occult practices

First known use: 1715

I can understand why some of you are thinking more of the second
definition. I watched *The Craft* too, and it is indeed super-fun watching
the girls change their eye color, their hair color, and sometimes even
their entire faces. But here's a spoiler: they had a special-effects department hard at work to make it look effortless.

I suppose if you had decided to give up television, or video games,
or whatever your dirty-little-secret time-waster happens to be, you

could truly work on definition 2. I would even say it's possible that with enough time, effort, and energy, you could get other people to believe your illusion.

I will ask you, however, which seems like a better use of your time: (a) spending a decade or so learning to change the color of your eyes, or (b) figuring out what qualities you actually possess that are very exciting and attractive to your optometrist so that she will be inclined to give you a discount on colored contacts, bringing them into your price range.

I'm still working, like, three jobs, so I would pick b. Maybe you have much more time in your day to devote to appearance-based illusions, and if you do and that's your jam, far be it from me to keep you from such lofty occult-driven pursuits. I have to be completely honest: I don't understand why people think they don't need glamour magic as part of their personal practice. But then again, most people, in my experience as a shopkeeper, think they don't need love magic either.

I don't understand why people think they don't need glamour magic as part of their personal practice. But then again, most people, in my experience as a shopkeeper, think they don't need love magic either.

I'm totally a naughty pony about love magic too. I'm very quick to wave my hand dismissively and say what all my clients say: "I already have love, thank you." It's such a ridiculous thing to say, isn't it? It's like saying, "My relationship is so incredibly perfect right now that nothing you could offer me could improve it. What do I need with more incredible sex, more money so we fight even less, a more compatible schedule so we actually see each other, more dates where we can focus on each other, and more long, lazy mornings in bed that slide into brunch? No! I don't need any of that!"

I got really interested in glamour for a few reasons: (a) No one talks about it and almost no one writes about it; (b) it's not something that comes naturally to me, and after observing others in the wild, I would say that it really only comes naturally to maybe one in ten people (here's a hint: it's probably not natural to you either); (c) once you get the hang of it, it's a quick-working kind of magic; and (d) I can tell when it's working.

How to Be Glamorous

To be effectively glamorous, you need to have a few things going for you:

1. You Need to Look Put Together.

Put together doesn't always mean J.Crew, but it does mean that other people can tell that you put some effort into how you look. I know that sounds vague, and it's intentionally so. Does it look like you got dressed in the dark, or does it look like you coordinated an outfit? Does it look like you take care of your face in some way, or does it look like you've never washed or moisturized? Does your hair look styled or like you just rolled out of bed (and not in a sexy way)?

I can feel myself losing about half of you here already. Here's a hard truth: You are being judged regularly by how you look, just like you're judging the rest of the world by how they look. I can tell you that I get treated very differently now than I did when I was heavier, dressed in sweats, with my hair up in a ratty ponytail. We can cry about how the world isn't fair or we can use what we have to our advantage. Witchcraft has always been the tool of the disadvantaged to even the playing field in an unfair world. Your appearance is one more tool in your occult toolbox. Don't throw that tool on the ground. There are lots of well-coiffed people of all sizes, shapes, and genders.

2. You Need to Have Your Life Put Together.

People are fascinated by train wrecks, of course, but after a while most people slowly back away from them. It's okay to be going through a rough patch, but if someone hasn't died recently, you're making enough money to pay your bills, and you're not going through a divorce, then... pull it together. Magic will not single-handedly pull your life together. You need to do that, sport. I mean, it would be totally great if it did, but that has not been my experience. Having your life together doesn't mean Miss Martha (Stewart) perfection; it means that you have a handle on your job, your body, your living space, your relationships, and any small children or animals that are in your charge. Once you're more effective at that, magic will help you get that much closer to accomplishing whatever you're trying to achieve. Here's a good question to ask: Do people come to you for assistance in various aspects of life because they admire how you are managing your own, or are people more inclined to ask you if you need help? If you're getting more offers of assistance than requests for help, then you need to get it together.

3. You Need to Have Some Genuine Confidence about 1 and 2.

Not bravado. Confidence. Bravado: telling people how awesome you are, how great your life is, how often people find you attractive: *Look at my car/purse/girlfriend.* Confidence: *I don't need to tell you any of those things. I already know it and I'm showing it just by showing up and having those things. If you don't notice, that's fine. I know.*

4. Glamour Is Easy When You're in That Halcyon Age Group of 16 to 25.

When you're in this age group, the rest of the world wants to believe that you're beautiful and talented, so it's easy enough to go along with it. Your hair is shiny, so skin blemishes are overlooked; your figure is likely the best it will ever be, so no one cares about your small imperfections; and your fashion sense seems gamine and charming no matter how much eyeliner and glitter you smear on yourself. (I'm looking at you too, boys and non-binary-gender people. You know who you are.) You are filled with unlimited potential. You could be a singer, a writer, a dancer, an artist, or whatever you want to be. You don't care about living conditions much anyway, as long as there's booze and friends. Living off ramen and popcorn is chic as long as there are chopsticks.

As long as you're young, you'll be beautiful. As long as there's a tomorrow, you'll always have time to fulfill all of that potential your family and high school teachers saw in you. *Today for you, tomorrow for me*, right? Eventually you wake up and that's not cute anymore. Enjoy it while you have it—use your glamour as leverage for whatever you're trying to accomplish. Dream big. When you wake up and you're twenty-six (or older!), however, you don't stop needing to accomplish whatever it is you're trying to accomplish. People will be less inclined to help you because you have so much unfulfilled potential and you are just a charming blank canvas for them to paint on, so that's when you need to be clear with yourself about which lines on your canvas are interesting and exciting and why.

5. True Glamour Is More Than Lipstick, More Than Bottle Service at the Club, More Than What Others Think of You.

It's easy to stop there, because those are the easy parts. Those are the parts that the media want you to care about. If you're always chasing the dragon (youth, what was, what never was), you take your eyes off the ball and what's actually important. When you are at your darkest, lowest point, when you feel like you're a dried-up husk with nothing left, when you feel like you have no new tricks, when you feel like you'll never be anything of worth, when you feel like you'll always struggle just to pay the damn electricity bill, when you feel like you can't remember what lust feels like or what it means to find something beautiful—that's when you go into your bathroom and turn out

all the lights and lay your head against the floor and hold the darkest, most powerful mirror up to yourself and look at what you see reflected back. Does it scare you? It should.

There are two types of glamour rooted in you: (1) the glamour you built on a lie and on wishing the world was different from what it actually is and wishing you were different from the way you actually are, and (2) the glamour built from your own personal truth, from accepting the world around you as it is right now and knowing everything dark and bright that lives inside you. Which one will be critical to your own evolution?

Yeah, the hard way is always the answer to getting someplace. But let's be real: most people don't want to do the work. But what does that mean?

It means that when you can take a good, hard, real look at yourself and the world you live in, you can figure out what you really want and what you're really capable of achieving for yourself. Once you figure out what you want, you can figure out how to do the mundane and magical work to get there. Sometimes doing the work isn't enough to get there. Sometimes even doing the magic on top of the work isn't enough—even after you stop getting in your own way, even

When you can take a good, hard, real look at yourself and the world you live in, you can figure out what you really want and what you're really capable of achieving for yourself. Once you figure out what you want, you can figure out how to do the mundane and magical work to get there.

after you get brave and pursue the things you most desire, and even if you have help.

The extra push is when you can build your personal glamour around you like a croquembouche's spun-sugar cage. The magic and the work is the croquembouche dessert itself. The spun-sugar cage is the glamour. You need the whole trifecta to push yourself forward in the world we live in right now. What makes *you* exciting and attractive? What is the spell that you cast on the rest of the world that says *look at me, damn it!* Once you have found that personal truth for yourself, build everything in your life around expressing that truth—your career, your home, your family life, your social life, your love life, your art, your magic, your appearance, everything.

Look. At. Me.

There is glamour in the darkness, in the evil queen, in the witch in the woods. There's something exciting about feathers, bones, and blood draped over a dark cloak and wild hair. Equally exciting is the dashing paladin, the good witch, the beloved queen. The beauty of the glittering armor, the jeweled crown, the drying herbs that smell of life and love … all of those things live inside you. But we tend to favor one over the other. Why? If you have command over both aspects and can have them married to each other within you, think of the power you could wield! There is a deep power in having an intimate knowledge of the aspects of yourself that most people shy away from. When you know the great and terrible things you are capable of, you know what lives inside of you. Think of the savage beauty that would come from that knowledge, the wild glamour that would shine from you with all the brightness of the sun and moon. What couldn't you accomplish?

Ritual: Rose Red, Rose White

This ritual will help you invoke your own personal glamour so you can access it for future spellcraft. You will need the following items:

- 1 cup spring water
- A clear glass bowl
- 1 tablespoon rose water
- 1 tablet of charcoal
- A heat-safe bowl
- 1 tablespoon dried lavender
- Whatever you need for trance work
- 1 white candle
- A mala bracelet (or your fingers)
- A sketchbook or notepad and sketch/writing implements
- 1 white rose
- 1 red candle
- 1 red rose

Pour the spring water in the bowl and bless it with your intention to activate your glamour. Add the rose water and bless that with your intention as well. Light the charcoal in a heat-safe bowl and put the dried lavender on it, and let the smoke flow over you. Get into a trance space using whatever methods you usually use (such as counting your breaths, imagining that you are growing roots into the ground and branches into the sky, or dancing until your brain shifts).

Light the white candle and focus on finding the light aspects of your glamour, the parts of you that are considered positive. Chant *Om mani padme hum* ("Praise to the jewel in the lotus") either eighteen or 108 times, whichever is more comfortable for you. Use the bracelet or your fingers to keep track. Be sure to use your thumb and middle fingers to pass the beads, not your pointer finger. Write down or sketch the aspects that come to you. Put one white rose petal in the bowl for each aspect. Take a moment to consider how you can internalize this part of your glamour.

Light the red candle and focus on finding the darker aspects of your glamour, the parts of you that are considered negative. Follow the same procedure as you did for the light side, this time using red rose petals.

When you are ready to open your glamour to yourself and to the universe, plunge your hands into the water and then pass your wet hands over the top of your head. Sit with this for a moment. Write or sketch whatever comes to you during this time. Let the candles burn out. And so it is.

Deborah Castellano's *first book,* Glamour Magic: The Witchcraft Revolution to Get What You Want, *is now available for your reading pleasure. Deborah is a frequent contributor to occult/Pagan sources such as the Llewellyn annuals, PaganSquare, and* Witches & Pagans *magazine, and she blogs at* Charmed, I'm Sure (www.charmedfinishingschool.com). *Her shop, the Mermaid and the Crow, specializes in handmade goods. She resides in New Jersey with her husband, Jow, and their cat. She has a terrible reality television habit she can't shake and likes St. Germain liqueur, record players, and typewriters.*

Illustrator: Kathleen Edwards

How to Use the Wheel of the Year as a Daily Practice

Dr. Alexandra Chauran

The wheel of the year is a Wiccan term for how the calendar of seasonal events looks when laid out as a wheel with eight spokes. Four of the spokes are made up of the two equinoxes and two solstices, and the remaining spokes of the wheel are other agricultural and pastoral holidays. Celebrating the wheel of the year can help you get your body in sync with Mother Nature and also understand metaphorically how life moves in cycles and seasons.

If you are already celebrating things like a winter holiday that brings cheer to dark, cold times or a harvest holiday that makes use of the bounty of the earth, you're partway there. However, I find that some beginners experience confusion with the wheel of the year. Trying to fit new holidays into a busy schedule feels more like a chore than a practice that connects us with mindfulness and spirit. If you're not totally familiar with the wheel of the year, it might feel a bit disingenuous each time you decorate your altar for a different holiday. However, the learning curve for a new follower of the wheel of the year is a long one. Each brand-new set of seasonal practices happens only once a year. So how can you start loving the wheel of the year as if you grew up with it as a child? Begin practicing the wheel of the year as a daily devotional.

Steps for Practicing the Wheel of the Year Daily

Step 1: At sunrise, or as soon as you get up if after sunrise, wash your body or your face and face east to greet the sun. Speak words of prayer that you would say at Ostara, the time of growth and rebirth.

Step 2: Mid-morning, perhaps when driving to work, sing a song of joy and connection, as if celebrating Beltane.

Step 3: At noon, face north and say a sort of grace over your lunch, giving thanks for the bounty of the earth.

Step 4: In the afternoon, express gratitude for the harvest that you have received in your life and for what you have been given this day. Say prayers and meditate on the festival of Lammas.

Step 5: At sunset, thank the God of the sun for being with you this day, rewarding you with food and other harvests. Observe the light as it fades and know that it shall return with a new day.

Step 6: At bedtime, face southwest and pray for the spirits of the ancestors to give you wisdom and guard you as you sleep.

Step 7: If you awaken during the night, think of this as your date with the gods and, facing south, say loving prayers to them in gratitude for keeping you company during the night.

Prayer Cheat Sheet for Your Book of Shadows

Time of Day	Direction	Prayer Theme
Sunrise	East	Ostara
Morning	Northeast	Beltane
Noon	North	Litha
Afternoon	Northwest	Lammas
Sunset	West	Mabon
Night	Southwest	Samhain
Midnight	South	Yule
Note that Imbolc is missing because it would take place before you wake up in the morning, and so it takes place during the dream time.		

Traditional Wiccan Practice

For a concrete example of how to observe the wheel of the year in traditional Wiccan practice, let's begin at the beginning of the day, at sunrise (or as soon as I wake), which is associated with the east. In my traditional Wiccan practice, I believe that at least the priestesses are obligated to face east and light a candle while kneeling at an altar and reciting the words typically said by the High Priestess at Ostara. I do this at a family altar in my house, and it certainly feels like lighting the hearth fire to get the day moving.

Between sunrise and noon, a Beltane prayer can be sung, while driving to work or doing chores or at an altar. At noon, Litha prayers can be spoken, and additional prayers added according to need.

Between sunrise and noon, a Beltane prayer can be sung, while driving to work or doing chores or at an altar. At noon, Litha prayers can be spoken, and additional prayers added according to need. Between noon and sunset, I believe that at least the priests should say the Lammas prayer as representatives of the God in his mythological dying time on the wheel of the year. At sunset, a Mabon prayer should be spoken while watching the setting sun if possible, at least by the priestesses. In the evening, the Samhain prayer can be said either at dinner or at bedside. Finally, a Yule prayer can be said at midnight, or just before closing eyes to sleep if before midnight, by the priests at least.

Tips and Tricks for Fitting the
Wheel of the Year into Your Day

The previous examples apply to my practice, but you can tweak them to work in the context of your life. If you're a solitary Wiccan priestess or priest, by Jove, you can go right ahead and say all the prayers yourself. If you typically vary the words you say during sabbats, pick your favorite words to say, and try keeping just one or more prayers the same as your daily prayers to start triggering those memories and keys to your subconscious daily connection with your gods.

Such a prayer clock may seem like a stretch for us modern folk, but saying prayers at those times was common for people in agrarian cultures who arose at dawn. Having only one eight-hour chunk of sleep at night is a relatively new shift in behavior, brought about by modern lighting. Even the rich would not burn candles to stay up late every

night for no reason in times past, so sleep was usually begun earlier in the evening and punctuated by a period of quiet wakefulness in the middle of the night. Christian writings are replete with prayers that were spoken near midnight, during a period of wakefulness. My own experience with choosing to speak the Yule prayer when awake at midnight has helped soothe me to sleep. While I once hated waking in the middle of the night, I now think of it as my date with the gods; they wake me whenever they need me and know I need them.

Reviving obligatory prayer practices is highly beneficial to Wiccan practice. Committing to the discipline of a daily routine helps the body and the mind relish in daily and seasonal cycles. Reciting prayers aids memorization for those of us who use traditional rituals, and makes the brain accustomed to saying the sacred words during a time of day that corresponds with the season. When all Wiccans make these associations, covens become more of a cohesive, single mind during worship. I like to imagine that repeated rituals create a comforting and familiar path in the collective unconscious of humankind, like a deep wheelbarrow rut on a dirt road. Likewise, the unity of all Wiccans is strengthened by the knowledge that, for those who choose to take on obligatory prayer, we are united in prayer to turn the wheel. Even if you're a solitary Wiccan, you can act as a team and only do the daily prayers that you feel are appropriate to your role as priestess or priest, with the faith that your fellow Wiccans have the rest covered. If you're up at midnight, it helps

Reviving obligatory prayer practices is highly beneficial to Wiccan practice. Committing to the discipline of a daily routine helps the body and the mind relish in daily and seasonal cycles.

to know you're not the only one finding comfort in worship. Finally, daily obligatory prayers form a backbone of solitary devotions that are at the heart of establishing a Wiccan worldview.

Bibliography

al-Bukhari, Muhammad. *Sahih al-Bukhari.*

Baha'u'llah. *Kitab-i-Aqdas.*

Carmichael, Alexander. *Carmina Gadelica.*

Hegarty, Stephanie. "The Myth of the Eight-Hour Sleep." BBC World Service, February, 22, 2012. www.bbc.co.uk/news/magazine-16964783.

Leland, Charles Godfrey. *Aradia, or The Gospel of the Witches.*

Qur'an.

Dr. Alexandra Chauran (Issaquah, WA) *is a second-generation fortuneteller, a High Priestess of British Traditional Wicca, and the Queen of a coven. As a professional psychic intuitive for over a decade, she serves psychic apprentices and thousands of clients. She received a master's degree in teaching from Seattle University and a doctorate from Valdosta State University, and is certified in tarot. In her spare time, when she's not teaching students of Wicca, she enjoys ham radio with the call sign WI7CH. She can be found online at SeePsychic.com.*

Illustrator: Rik Olson

Witchcraft Essentials

PRACTICES, RITUALS & SPELLS

Spell-Check

James Kambos

If you've ever watched reruns of the TV sitcom *Bewitched*, you've probably seen Samantha's sweet but bumbling Aunt Clara. Try as she might, Aunt Clara's spells just never seemed to work. Her spells would go awry and the results were always hilarious.

Of course, that was Hollywood. In real life, when a spell doesn't work out as planned, it's no laughing matter. It leaves you feeling frustrated, at the very least. Believe me, the most experienced magical practitioners, myself included, have cast spells that didn't work or didn't turn out as hoped for. Then there have been times when a spell did work, but I didn't realize it at the time.

When a spell doesn't bring the desired result, first of all and most importantly, don't start blaming yourself. Instead, slow down, take a deep breath, and analyze the spell. Retrace your steps to see where you might have gone off track. To do this you need to look at each step in the spell process. When I do this type of spell assessment, I refer to it as a "spell-check."

A spell-check can take time, but it's time well spent. It can turn your next spell into a huge success and prevent another dud.

The Spell-Check Process

Casting a spell isn't just saying some words and then hoping that the desired change comes to you. Spell work should be a well-thought-out

step-by-step plan, so that when you need to do a spell-check, you'll be able to go back to each step and check what you did. This is how you may find a mistake you made.

What follows is the spellcasting plan I use, broken into simple steps. Your spell structure may be different—that's okay. For each step, I explain what you should do as you prepare and cast a spell. But, more importantly, I point out typical mistakes that people make during each step. Hopefully, after reading my suggestions, you'll be able to avoid these pitfalls, and your spells will work more smoothly.

STEP ONE: THE GOAL

A spell is like a building: it needs a good foundation. Step one is the spell's foundation, when you decide what you want. This is your goal or purpose. It's critical for you to determine the one thing you want from this spell. Notice I said "one thing." Here is where many people make the mistake of asking for more than one outcome. What is it you really want? A new home or a new car? A raise or a new job?

During this first step, you should decide what you want and state it precisely, even if you only think it. If you don't decide on your goal now, and how you want your wish to come to you, your spell will be hit or miss at best.

It's critical for you to determine the one thing you want from this spell. Notice I said "one thing." Here is where many people make the mistake of asking for more than one outcome. What is it you really want?

Step Two: Preparation

The second step is usually when I prepare for the spell. This is when you make sure you have all the supplies you'll need. If you'll need a certain color of fabric or candle, now is the time to make sure you have it. Will you need a certain herb or plant material? Check your kitchen or garden to make certain you have these available. Remember, the proper spell ingredients will add energy and power to your spell. They'll also put you in the proper frame of mind when you cast the spell. Now isn't the time to skip a critical spell ingredient. Doing so will weaken the spell's outcome.

However, it's all right to substitute certain ingredients if they'll give the same results. I recommend becoming familiar with the magical powers of herbs and plants first, before you begin exchanging one herb for another in a spell.

There will be times when you have to make do with what you have on hand. For example, if you need snow but you live in Key West, then naturally you can use ice instead.

During this second step, you should also make sure all your magical tools (such as a cauldron, magic mirror, etc.) are clean and ready to go if you think you may need them.

Not being prepared will scatter your energy, which could lead to a spell's failure.

Step Three: Timing

The timing of a spell can be critical to its success. When I say timing, I'm talking about things like the moon phase, planetary influences, and days of the week. An entire book could be devoted to this subject, but I'll try to keep it simple.

Farmers have always understood that activities like planting, cultivating, and pruning are best done during the proper moon phase.

This is also true of spellcasting. Working magic during the correct moon phase will increase your chances of success.

Here are the moon phases I work with and how I use them for spellcasting:

- **Dark Moon:** During this phase, the moon is not visible in the sky. Use this phase for meditation and spell preparation. Spells to break bad habits can be cast now.

- **New Moon:** When the first sliver of moon appears after the dark moon, it's the new moon. Now is a good time to determine a goal for a spell. Casting spells for self-improvement, a job search, or a new home can be done now.

- **Waxing Moon**: During this phase, the moon is increasing in size, becoming almost round. Spells should be performed

now to draw things to us, such as employment, abundance, and friendship.

- **Full Moon:** Now the moon is completely round. This is the moon's most powerful phase. Important spells for health, love, and legal matters should be cast now.

- **Waning Moon:** The moon's size and power begin to decrease now. Spells cast during this phase may include those intended to end things, such as relationships, habits, or any negative forces.

If you need a quick reference guide to moon phases and astrological influences, I suggest you get a current copy of *Llewellyn's Witches' Spell-A-Day Almanac*.

The day of the week on which you choose to cast a spell can also be important. Here is a brief guide. For spells concerning business, money, and good luck, I've found Sunday, Wednesday, and Thursday to be favorable. If your spell has to do with home and family, Monday is a good choice. For spells concerning legal matters, power, and protection, casting the spell on Tuesday will give you an edge. Love and friendship spells are best done on Friday. On Saturday, it's best to do banishing spells or break-a-habit spells.

As you can see, connecting a spell's theme with a particular moon phase or day of the week can create powerful magic.

Step Four: Words of Power

This is the step where you'll write or state your Words of Power. Words of Power are the written and spoken words of a charm or spell. They are the core of any spell. These words should be a positive affirmation of your desire. It doesn't need to be long, but it does need to be clear and direct. Words of Power may be directed to God, Goddess, Divine Power, or a specific deity.

Here is a sample of some Words of Power for a new home:

Divine Power, I affirm that
the perfect new home is coming into my life.
This home will be in the perfect location,
and it will be the perfect price.
This home will be perfect for my family.
My new home is coming to me now,
with perfect speed and ease.
It's coming to me with harm to none,
for the good of all, and free will of all.
So it must be.

These Words of Power are simple and to the point. They cover all the bases without time constraints. They affirm your wish without being demanding, and request that no one be harmed or forced to do anything against their free will.

These Words of Power are simple and to the point. They affirm your wish without being demanding, and request that no one be harmed or forced to do anything against their free will.

Here are some other things to remember about spell writing so you don't have any problems. Keep your language strong but positive. Don't use phrases such as "I hope so" or "Please let this happen." Never, ever write a spell in a language that you don't fully understand—who knows what you might conjure up? Also, don't put a specific person's name in a spell unless that person gives you permission.

After checking your Words of Power for any flaws, it's time for the final step: casting the spell.

Step 5: Cast the Spell

Now everything should come together. To avoid any issues getting your spell off the ground, have everything ready during this final step.

Your altar, for example, should be set up. Will you need music? If so, have it ready. Distractions are usually the main cause of failure at this point. If you're working alone, make sure your phone is turned off. If it's a coven spell, make sure before you begin that everyone agrees on the spell's goal. If they don't, the spell won't work.

Make sure you are grounded. Speak your Words of Power with confidence. Visualize the spell working, and release the spell.

It's done.

Some Final Thoughts

After casting a spell, get rid of any doubt that it will work. Also, don't think that you don't deserve your wish. This kind of thinking will "call back" a spell and prevent it from working in the Unseen Realm.

Be open to the spell working in a slightly different way. For example, I once cast a spell to sell my art at an exhibit. I sold nothing. Then after the exhibit was over, a gentleman looked me up and bought one of my paintings. He said he'd seen my work at the exhibit. So the spell *did* work. Sometimes the Divine Power knows what is best.

Once a spell works, show your gratitude. Simply saying thank you is enough. This will create good karma so that other spells may work.

When you have trouble getting a spell to work, remember: believe and you will receive!

James Kambos *is a writer and an artist. He developed an interest in folk magic as a child after seeing his grandmother cast spells.*

Illustrator: Bri Hermanson

Making and Using Witch Stones

Charlie Rainbow Wolf

Witch *stones*. You choose a stone and it tells you your future. It all sounds very intriguing, doesn't it? But what are they, exactly? Does every witch have the same needs and desires, and do they all use the same stones? There are quite possibly many answers to those questions.

What Witch Stones Are and What They Are Not

First, let's take a look at what they are *not*. Witch stones are not magic. How can they be? They're just lines on rocks. They

aren't runes. Rune stones are an alphabet, and while many witches use rune stones, the two shouldn't be confused. They're not crystals. It's possible to make witch stones from crystals, sure, but witch stones are more than just pretty pebbles. Witch stones won't take away your free will and they can't make you do anything you don't want to do. Also, the advice that witch stones share with you is, well, it's not carved in stone (you may groan out loud if you wish!). So just what are they?

Witch stones span different cultures and belief systems and aren't used only by witches. They are messengers. They help you to reach into your unconscious and bring forth ideas that you may not have considered before. They also tune in to the vibe of the universe, presenting you with concepts and potential outcomes to contemplate.

Witch stones are companions. When you need to talk things over with someone and there's no one around, use your witch stones! This is particularly helpful if you write down your question, consult the stones, and then note the answer. Often one dialogue will lead to further questions, different viewpoints, and other paths to explore. By keeping records of these conversations, you can review them from time to time and see how things are evolving.

Necessary Materials

Here's what you'll need to make your own witch stones.

Rocks or Stones

Choose whatever rocks or stones appeal to you. They'll need to be smooth so you can paint on them. The usual number in a set of witch stones is thirteen, for a myriad of reasons. If you wish to add more stones with symbols on them, go ahead—these are your stones and there's no hard and fast rule. You might also want to get more stones than you need in case you mess one up and choose to discard and redo it. Something else to consider is having a few blank spares, should you want to add more symbols as you get proficient at working with your stones.

Paint or Markers

Again, it doesn't matter which you use. If you choose paint, don't forget a paintbrush—and also cleaning materials to clear up any spills or mistakes you make.

Sealant

You've worked hard to make your stones, and you don't want the images to fade the first few times you use them. Use spray-on or brush-on sealant in a matte or gloss finish. The choice is yours, but see the previous note about cleaning up if you select the brush-on type.

A Flat Surface and Something to Cover It

Paint and sealant have the potential to get very messy. It's a good idea to put paper on your work surface or even work outside, especially when sealing your stones.

A Bag, Box, or Pouch for Storage

You will need a bag, box, or pouch (or the materials to make one) to store the stones in, and a cloth to put your stones on when laying them out to read.

Symbol Meanings

The first set of witch stones that I bought at a festival over twenty years ago had the following symbols: crossroads, eye, flight, harvest, man, moon, rings, romance, scythe, star, sun, waves, and woman.

They weren't elaborate images. The representation for woman was the letter Y, while the symbol for man looked like an arrow. There's no hard and fast rule, though; if you've got different designs or even different meanings that you want to include on your stones, do so. This is going to be your tool, so it needs to speak your language.

These images were chosen because of the universal messages they conveyed. There's no point in having a divination system that leaves you feeling confused or needing more from it, so even though these are the symbols usually used on witch stones, it's all open to interpretation. If you want to paint a tree to represent harvest, I'm certainly not going to tell you that you can't—and if anyone else says that, don't listen to them.

Crossroads

You've probably heard people speak about being at a crossroads in their lives; that is exactly what this stone embodies. There's a choice

to make, and it's probably not going to be an easy one. People reveal their true colors and may not be the friends you thought they were. It's time to reassess the situation and get your priorities sorted. While this stone is an indication of troubled times, it's also a promise that there are better days ahead.

EYE

If you think this stone means to watch where you're going, you're right! It's advising you to keep your eyes peeled and really see what's around you. Keep an eye on things that are important to you. Open your third eye and pay attention to your dreams and hunches. Observation is crucial, for you might overlook something important, something that has significance later on.

FLIGHT

Like birds gliding through the sky, you're about to overcome what's been holding you back and rise to new heights. This can represent breaking free of a restrictive situation, or unexpected good news that makes your heart soar. If you've been looking for signs and omens to guide you forward, they're being sent to you—and this is one of them! Communication and divine guidance are favored.

HARVEST

This is a very positive stone to pull in a reading, but it does come with a caveat. If you've been paying your dues and learning your lessons, you're going to be richly rewarded. If you've been shirking your responsibilities or trying to cut corners, you're likely to reap a reward of a different kind. Harvest is karma, and karma is the law of cause and effect. Usually this stone is a good omen—a very good one—but don't take it for granted.

Man

This stone implies power and force. Where the woman symbol relates to all aspects of the feminine archetype, man refers to the assertiveness of male energy. It's pushy and sometimes arrogant in nature, and it won't go down without a fight. Pay attention: this stone could be a warning that you're being coerced or that you're about to act on a whim that has the potential to land you in hot water.

Moon

Things might not all be what they seem when the moon witch stone is around. Shadows look more ominous at night than in the light of day, and it's easier to be deluded in the darkness than in the sun. This stone tells you to listen to your hunches and to pay attention to the natural cycle of things but to remember to have at least one foot grounded and objective.

Rings

It's probably not a surprise that seeing the rings stone usually involves commitment and contracts. There's teamwork here, and potential partnerships. Those partnerships could be of an intimate nature, such as a lover or a spouse, but rings can indicate business alliances too. The surrounding stones often give more clues, right down to an indication that some kind of bond needs to be severed.

Romance

This is a completely different symbol from the rings, and while some of the general nuances overlap, they shouldn't be confused. It's possible to be in love with your pastimes and hobbies, your work, and life itself. This stone doesn't necessarily mean you're romancing a person, but of course it can. Look at it as an indication that you need to be manifesting your bliss, finding your heart's desire, and pursuing your passion.

Scythe

Like the sharpest knife, the scythe is asking you to cut away what's not working. This might not be the most pleasant task to undertake, but it is a necessary one. When this stone appears, it's showing you that you're carrying baggage or that something in your life has run its course. To step into better times, you have to cut something—or someone—free. If you're going through challenges, the scythe is reassurance that you've got what it takes to cut through the obstacles and emerge victorious.

Star

Remember Jiminy Cricket singing "When You Wish Upon a Star" to Pinocchio in the Disney film? That's still the message of the star stone. Your wishes are about to come true. Of course, this stone does demand that you make the effort to turn those dreams into a reality. A goal without action remains just a wish. Expect the best, but be prepared to do some grunt work too.

Sun

Just like the tarot card of the same name, the sun witch stone brings a message of happiness and hope. It indicates a breakthrough, a changing of events, and a positive outcome. It points to a new beginning of some sort, perhaps embarking on a new quest or starting some kind of a new phase in your life. There's real abundance coming your way when the sun is in your stones, but remember that wealth isn't always about material possessions.

Waves

This stone indicates some kind of a journey. This could be literal, as in taking a trip, or metaphorical, as in journeying to new perceptions and a deeper awareness. In either case, it's nothing trivial. If the journey is physical, it will be lengthy or perhaps quite an upheaval—a foreign holiday or a house move, for example. If the journey is symbolic, then remain objective and don't let delusions lure you into a false sense of security. This is also a very creative stone. Some of the best ideas are the product of an active imagination.

WOMAN

While the woman symbol sometimes refers to an actual person in your life, it's more likely that it's pertaining to the feminine archetype. Creativity, sensitivity, nurturing, mothering, fertility, intuition, receptivity—these are all words that should be associated with this glyph, and I'm sure you can think of even more. There's great feminine energy in this stone, and its presence shouldn't be taken lightly.

Making and Storing the Stones

You now have an idea of what symbols to put on your stones, and you've gathered the necessary materials to make them. All that's needed now is your creativity! Before you dive in with the images, though, you might want to consider the timing. These are going to be a magical tool, so choose when to make them so that they bond easily with you and resonate strongly with your energy. I like to make mine during a lunar return. This is the time of the month when the moon is in the same sign and at the same degree in the skies as it was when you was born—even better if it's a new or full moon. Your birthday or a sabbat would also be a good time. There's no right or wrong way to do this; it's your intent that's important.

When I started making my own witch stones, I altered the images to suit my own symbolism, so feel free to do the same. Remember, these are just symbols, tried and tested and included because they work. Once you've chosen the symbols you want to use, paint them onto your stones, let the paint (or marker) dry, then seal them with an appropriate sealant. When they're completely dry (and some sealants take a while, so leave them out and undisturbed for a day or two so they're not sticky), put them in a box or pouch for safe storage. It's a good idea to make the container for your stones, if possible, so that everything resonates with your energy, but it's not necessary.

Using the Stones

There's no definitive way to make the stones, and there's more than one way to use them, too. Pose your question and then draw a single stone for a short, sharp answer. Draw two stones for an either-or reading, to help you weigh your options, or to show you the potential outcomes of two different choices.

My favorite is the three-stone reading. Lay three stones on a flat surface or casting cloth, and read the stones from left to right. The left stone shows what is hindering you, the middle stone shows what is helping you, and the right stone shows the potential outcome. The three-stone layout can also be used for a past-present-future reading.

They're your stones and it's your reading, so assign whatever meanings you wish to use. The only rule here is consistency. Don't change the meanings of the positions halfway through the reading simply because you don't like what you see!

. . . .

Once you've made your first set of witch stones, you might want to experiment with other mediums. Polymer clay is used a lot. Being a ceramic artist, I make mine in stoneware and fire them in the kiln. If pyrometry is your thing, you could burn the images onto wooden disks. I can't stress enough that there's no one right way to do this, so get creative. Soon you'll find that you have more than just a divination tool: the stones are an ally, a counselor, and a guide, right at your fingertips!

Charlie Rainbow Wolf *is happiest when she is creating something, especially if it can be made from items that others have cast aside. Pottery, writing, knitting, astrology, and tarot are her deepest interests, but she happily confesses that she's easily distracted because life offers so many wonderful things to explore. She is an advocate of organic gardening and cooking and lives in the Midwest with her husband and special-needs Great Danes. Visit her at www.charlierainbow.com.*

Illustrator: Jennifer Hewitson

Scrying Made Easy: Using Everyday Objects to Build Your Skill

Michael Furie

Tales of ancient seers gazing into the unknown by means of a crystal ball or through the seemingly infinite depths of a black mirror or water-filled cauldron can create such romantic notions of the ancient art of scrying that it may seem ethereal and out of reach. Far from being a rare gift bestowed upon a select few, scrying is actually a magical skill that we each possess and experience unconsciously with relative regularity. To cultivate this talent, the standard advice usually suggests obtaining a suitable scrying mirror, crystal ball, or bowl of water to use as a gazing medium and also to develop a regular practice of meditation to help condition the mind. While these are sound suggestions, I feel they can also be impediments if a person does not have the free time for meditation or the means to obtain the requisite tools. It's important to keep in mind that in order for any type of magic, divination, or spiritual work to be relevant in our lives, it should be accessible and workable. We need not confine ourselves to narrow guidelines that don't meet our needs; creativity is the key that can open the way to numerous scrying possibilities.

When I first started learning to scry about twenty years ago, I modified a picture frame to make a flat black mirror to use and had little to no results with my creation. I blamed my "failure" on a lack of proper materials and decided that scrying might not be for me. It wasn't until a couple of years later that I accidentally began to scry again. I wasn't feeling well, so I decided to lie down for a nap but instead found myself staring at the ceiling. Sunlight filtering through the window lit up the room, and as I gazed at the ceiling, for the first time ever images began to form. Granted, it wasn't as dramatic as the Wicked Queen from *Snow White* gazing into

her magic mirror, but at least progress was finally being made! My eyes were relaxed and the texture of the ceiling began to move as if it were melting. Then pictures started to appear.

Since what I was seeing didn't match the expectation I held for scrying, I failed to recognize what was happening as a budding talent, and instead wrote it off as a simple daydream. Everything I'd heard or read on the subject of scrying up until that point had led me to believe that either I would see only mental images or the visions would be so strong that they would appear almost as television images within whatever scrying tool I was using. These possibilities may be correct for some people, but neither was true for me. For the most part, what I saw were shapes of people, animals, and things that appeared to be formed in the ceiling, a bit like those pictures where you almost have to cross your eyes to see the 3-D image outline. Given the fact that I had yet to realize I was beginning to develop scrying ability, I assumed that I was just having an especially active daydream, and I put it out of my mind. A while later, I came across some other people's practices of scrying and it occurred to me that all of the real-world experiences others were sharing had similarities to my own brief episode, so I began a deeper exploration of the art.

As my progression gained momentum, I learned a few truths regarding any form of gazing divination (and magic in general). The first thing I learned was why my accidental scrying had worked when all other attempts had failed: because I had finally achieved an altered state of consciousness without any effort. Prior to this, my only encounters with altered states had been for magical and ritual visualization, with an emphasis on focusing on active concepts, ideas, and goals rather than creating a passive, receptive state. I was fortunate enough to have been given advice and instruction from others regarding magic in my formative witchy years, but when it came to scrying I was almost completely on my own. Trying to meditate my way into the proper frame of mind felt like a lost cause until I learned that my understanding of the whole "proper frame of mind" concept needed some adjustment. I think a much better (though less mystical) term for the mental shift needed for this type of divination would be "zoning out." I'm not knocking meditation; it's a valuable tool, but it can seem intimidating for some of us.

Scrying Methods

When I began to successfully scry, all I really had to do was relax, gaze at whatever I was using as a focus, and zone out. Though I didn't know it at the time, technically speaking I was allowing my mind to naturally shift into an altered state of consciousness known as alpha brainwave level. This is the same state we reach when we are first falling asleep; it is a receptive, more psychic level of awareness. Once my mind shifted, I could mentally ask questions and receive symbolic answers.

With this newfound understanding, my scrying attempts took on a whole new dimension. One of the easiest times for me to relax and zone out is when taking a hot bath or shower. Though this can be an ideal time for scrying, a steamy bathroom isn't the best location for a black mirror or a crystal ball. A surprisingly helpful substitute is to use a large bath towel in a solid color. I think it has something to do with the texture of the fabric; it gives the eyes something to focus on without too much effort. For me, a black towel works best, but any solid color can work. Relaxing in the tub and softly gazing at a towel hung flat on a towel rack can be a very effective means of divination. Generally speaking, the idea of using a solid, opaque item as a focus for gazing is not highly regarded; using an object with depth (such as a mirror or crystal) is often seen as superior. For some reason, though, the towel option works well for me. My theory is that the subtle texture provides enough of a surface to distract my conscious mind and give my subconscious room to flow. I've found that virtually any object can be used to scry as long as the coloring or pattern isn't too garish or distracting.

Another soothing scrying method can be used in the morning if you have a little free time. If you are a coffee or tea drinker, you can use these liquids as a gazing medium. Ideally, they should be in a plain cup or mug, and milk or cream should be omitted if you prefer a focus with depth. So many people, myself included, drink a cup of coffee or tea first thing in the morning to help shake off grogginess and start the day, and this is the perfect time for scrying. The brain is still in a slower, more reflective mode (at least until the caffeine kicks in), and this is the perfect mental state for scrying. Not only is this an excellent time to obtain strong results, but after you are finished your mind will be more alert, allowing you to remember and write down any messages received. To do this work before bed is more difficult even though the brain is in an alpha state at that time too, because there will be a tendency to fall asleep during or after and thus messages may be

forgotten before there is a chance to record them. Incidentally, if you prefer an uncaffeinated beverage for this work, decaffeinated coffee or tea is fine, as are herbal teas such as chamomile, though using a dark cup with a lighter drink would be best.

Another scrying option that made itself known to me when I was really bored and a bit sleepy is that of simply gazing at a surface made of dark wood, such as a tabletop or cabinet. If the wood has a rich color with a slight sheen to it, then it can be a surprisingly efficient scrying tool. Another more portable tool to use if you prefer a "Witches' mirror" but cannot locate a suitable version is to modify a coupe cocktail glass to serve as a substitute looking glass. The coupe is a type of glass that was used for champagne prior to the rise of the flute-style glass, and it was also used for cocktails before the modern martini-style cocktail glass became the standard. Coupe glasses are those wide-mouthed, shallow, "bowl on a stem" glasses. Occasionally you can find one made of black glass, but if all you can find is a clear one, simply paint the outside of the glass with flat black paint (coating it as many times as necessary so that no light shines through) and declare it to be your scrying glass. This creation can then be used either filled with water or by itself; just gaze into it and relax your mind.

If you prefer an outdoor divinatory experience, try settling beneath a shady tree and either stare up at the leaves or find a large leaf and hold it in your hands. Let your mind zone out and simply gaze, allowing the images or symbols to form. This method also helps you connect to the spirit of the tree and other local land spirits. To interact with nature spirit energies a bit farther away, cloud scrying can be a very effective practice. On a cloudy day, find a comfortable place to sit where you can gaze at the clouds and let your mind wander. Think of yourself as you are now, then mentally project your focus outward, up to the clouds, and ask whatever questions you may have. To gain your answers, observe the shapes the clouds form and also the direction in which they move.

Most answers are gained via symbols or images that need to be interpreted later to understand their meaning. This is why it is important to write down everything you see during a scrying session, because the true answer may take some time to uncover, depending on the nature of the symbols. Since this practice is so individualized, a single symbol can have a variety of meanings depending on the gazer. As an example, a spider appearing could signal danger to some people, but to others it could indicate the need for a more methodical approach to their work or home life. A book of dream or divination symbols can come in handy for this work, though your own intuition is the best interpreter. It is possible that at first only vague shapes will appear, such as clouds, or in the case of the ceiling method it may just seem like the texture of the ceiling is floating. This is fine. Ask a yes-no type of question and observe how the shapes react. Frequently, clouds or random shapes will travel upward to indicate a yes answer to a question and downward for a no; experiment to determine how they move for you.

. . . .

Even though scrying is a wondrous and magical activity, it also has a practical side that, for me, was the key to gaining this ability and refining it into a skill. There was too much of an ethereal, mystical quality attached to it at first. I eventually discovered that scrying is a simple, valuable, practical form of divination that can be used anywhere. Once I realized that the traditional tools were not mandatory, I was able to integrate scrying into my practice in ways that work for me. I hope these unorthodox methods will augment and expand traditional scrying practice and help show that sometimes the practical is the most mystical of all.

Michael Furie (*Northern California*) *is the author of* Spellcasting for Beginners, Supermarket Magic, Spellcasting: Beyond the Basics, *and more, all from Llewellyn Worldwide. A practicing Witch for more than twenty years, he is a priest of the Cailleach. He can be found online at* www.michaelfurie.com.

Illustrator: Tim Foley

Devotional Practice:
Caring for the Sacred Land

Stephanie Woodfield

If I could sum up the core, or perhaps the heart, of my practices, it would be devotion. Devotional practice is something we don't talk about enough in Paganism, and sometimes don't understand. It often is a deeply personal practice, and the way it is expressed from individual to individual can differ greatly—which is what makes devotional practice both beautiful and at times difficult to describe.

There are innumerable ways to honor the gods. For a long time I thought that all there was to devotional practice was prayers by my altar, offerings, incense, and so much poured wine, but devotional work is not always a tangible thing. Sometimes what the gods want is not incense or libations but our action.

Some of the most meaningful devotional work I have done is caring for sacred sites. A sacred site can be anything from an ancient site connected to the gods or particular spirits to your favorite spot in nature. Whether it's a circle of standing stones or a favorite tree in your backyard or local park, these places need tending. Caring for them can be both a rewarding experience and an offering to the divine.

This kind of stewardship of the land became a vital part of a pilgrimage to Ireland I was part of this past Samhain. In Ireland there are few places that don't have a story, god, or myth attached to them. There is even an entire text, the *Dindshenchas* (meaning "lore of places"), that details how many of the places in Ireland got their names, and the myths surrounding them. And so it was easy to imagine the myths of the Morrigan and the Irish gods taking place in the beautiful sites we visited. There were many moving experiences I was blessed with on that pilgrimage, but the one that struck me the most was visiting the triple spring at Ogulla. What are commonly called *wells* in Ireland are what we would call *springs*, with water naturally flowing up from the ground, often having been lined with stones at some point. This well was a small pool surrounded by trees, with a statue of Saint Patrick on a low stone wall beside it. Opposite the spring stood a small covered building with some Christian paraphernalia, which the pope had visited at some point.

At first the Ogulla well was not a site that I connected with strongly, at least not in the way one would expect. The day before the pilgrimage officially began, we visited both of Brigid's wells in Kildare, and I felt a strong connection to them. But this place felt different, tired. The well was clogged with overgrown weeds and water plants. Although we could see the water flowing away through a stone channel, it was hard to see the spring itself. After our guide told us a little about the spring,

we were asked to take a handful of weeds out of the water before we left as a way to care for this sacred place.

We ended up doing far more than that. I remember stooping down at the water's edge with a fellow pilgrim next to me, and we both tugged at what looked like a carpet of green that covered the surface of the water. We tugged and brought up small handfuls of weeds, but it didn't feel like enough. Together we reached out farther, and with a great tug that almost made me fall on my backside, a huge sheet of green ripped free and floated toward us. For the first time I could see the pool beneath the weeds. And from there it became everyone's mission to clear every weed and every bit of garbage from the well.

People pulled on their boots or waded in the water barefoot to tear up the weeds clogging the spring. We hauled armfuls of the plants behind a stone wall to be mulched, and soon it was piled higher than the wall itself. We pulled up garbage, CDs, tealights, and even a dead rosebush complete with plastic pot. Soon all the growth was cleared away and the water moved easily, and there was a very good feeling coming from the well and the land around it. Our guide told us that most people usually take only a single obligatory handful of weeds, and we all felt a sense of satisfaction that we had gone above and beyond. Later, more than one person mentioned that caring for the well had been a deeply profound experience for them. Caring for a sacred place, giving this act of devotion and love to the land, was deeply rewarding. I didn't receive any profound visions or messages from this place in particular, yet it was one of my favorite experiences from the trip.

During the rest of our trip we cut off all manner of insane things that people tied to the branches of trees over several other springs and at sacred mounds. The tradition of hanging *clooties*, or rags, on trees is an old one. In general the idea is that as the cloth rots away, the illness of a person will dissipate as well. Unfortunately, most of our modern-day fabrics do not biodegrade easily. We found many things on trees such as synthetic ribbons and hair ties, and when these are left there instead of eventually falling away, they can choke and kill the sacred trees.

On a more local level, I have always enjoyed being outside, and early in my devotional work I found I preferred walking meditations to ones sitting cross-legged at home. During the week I would spend most of the day behind a computer, so time spent outside moving my body, climbing trails in the woods, and offering my sweat to the gods seemed fitting. As a way to honor the land and the gods, I would also bring a small garbage bag in my backpack and stop to pick up any garbage I found, which unfortunately was oftentimes quite a lot. Eventually, caring for the land became an important aspect of my spirituality.

More often than not, we go to a place, be it a park or a sacred place, and have the expectation that something magickal and profound is going to happen to us. We go expecting blessings and gifts and don't always take time to consider what we can do for the spirit of the land or the god that is connected to that place. We go into the experience with our hands outstretched, ready to receive, and we forget that devotion doesn't always mean receiving. Sometimes devotional acts are more meaningful because of the act of giving without any expectation of receiving a blessing in return.

> **More often than not, we go to a place, be it a park or a sacred place, and have the expectation that something magickal and profound is going to happen to us. We go expecting blessings and gifts and don't always take time to consider what we can do for the spirit of the land or the god that is connected to that place.**

You may not be able to visit sacred sites in other countries, but a piece of land doesn't have to have had spiritual significance for thousands of years for it to be holy. I operate under the idea that all space is sacred space. That straggly, struggling tree on the side of the highway, the potted plant on your apartment balcony, the dog park down the road—all are sacred pieces of earth.

Practical Tips for Caring for a Sacred Place

If you want to do this kind of devotional work, choose a place near you that either you feel a close affinity to or you know has not been cared for very well. Spend time connecting to the place. Leave offerings either to the spirits of the land or to the gods you have a devotion to.

Here is a simple way to greet the land. Leave an offering of some kind, preferably something that would benefit the land, such as water,

seeds, etc. Place your hand on the ground (or if it's a tree, on the trunk, etc.) and say:

I greet the spirits of the land,
Those that live and have dominion over this holy space.
May there be peace between us.

Spend some time communing with the land. This could be quiet meditation or it could be walking around the area and enjoying its beauty. You may feel the presence of the spirit that inhabits that particular piece of land, or of the plant spirits or even the gods connected to it. I used to use a particular tree as a place where I would leave offerings that I felt were "used up" on my indoor altars. If an offering doesn't evaporate naturally or is something perishable like food, after a few days (or when I feel the deity is done with it, having taken the essence of the offering) I dispose of what is left. And this tree in particular is where I would leave these spent offerings. After a while I realized that when I was near the tree I would feel that deity's presence very strongly, and was even instructed by that deity to do particular kinds of rituals near or under the tree at one point. I had inadvertently made the tree a holy place for that god, and the deity in question seemed very fond of it, even to the point of the tree blooming longer than the other nearby plants. Its flowers would last longer than expected, and one year its leaves stayed green almost a month after the leaves on all the other trees had turned orange and red and fallen.

Once you have become acquainted with the spirits connected to the land you are tending, spend some time finding out what the land requires. What does it tell you? Does it need more water? Is there something invasive in the area that you can help it with (like the water plants choking the well at Ogulla)? Is there garbage you can pick up to keep the land clean?

Be creative in your approach to devotional work, and honor the land and the gods in all that you do. Honoring the gods involves far more than just offering them libations. Your work and actions can be an expression of living devotion.

Stephanie Woodfield *has been a practicing Pagan for the past twenty years. A devotional polytheist, ritualist, author, and Priestess of the Morrigan, she is one of the founding members of Morrigu's Daughter and the Morrigan's Call Retreat. She is called to help others forge meaningful experiences with the Morrigan as well as the gods and land of Ireland.*

Illustrator: Kathleen Edwards

How to Create a Magick Broom Cupboard

Estha McNevin

Living in the country, I often find myself in the company of those crafters who, by way of their art, mastery, and experience, are forever launching my aspiration for functional art right out of the stratosphere. One early afternoon in the dog days of summer, I had the pleasure of attending a workshop hosted by one such traditional broom maker, Maria Bullock, who teaches locally at the Cedar-Root Folk School. By learning the techniques and skills required for the craft, I came to fall in love with the many varieties and styles of esoteric and domestic brooms.

Rediscovering these amazing witchy tools, hewed with the true magickal artistry of functionality, has taught me how to stay more self-disciplined in my own habits. For me, the besom helps lift and clear more than just dust, especially when casting and receiving the regular magick within our temple house. Broom magick comforts, strengthens, and feeds positive spirits, including faeries and brownies, by marrying our naturalistic motifs, Pagan libations, and lucky offerings (like domestic spells) with our real-world goals. We base so many of these habits on the seasonal festivities because they call upon our shared social values.

In our small community-supported temple and farm, we are always fertilizing the tenacity of the living earth as a principal highland theme of our willful broom-based magick. This is profoundly expressed in the functional agrarian tools that we use every day, many of which are highly decorated with creative Pagan symbolism and doubly utilized in ceremony. This authentically draws lucky thoughts and invites playful out-of-doors nature spirits, who come with their positive intentions to aid us in our work.

A Besom by Any Name Is
an Instrument of Magick

Brooms are sacred symbols of agricultural spirituality for many reasons. They connect us to a very insightful method of harvesting in accordance with nature's cycles, of which some crops (like broom grasses) are an environmental indicator. Their decay marks subtle changes in seasonal conditions. As animists, we both worship and are beguiled by agricultural cycles because they evoke premonitions based on our innocent curiosity and wonder. In the modern world, perhaps we find ourselves turning with ever-increasing marvel to the old ways—which have long venerated grasses and trees—in part for the secret natural wisdom that they innately maintain.

The seasons and their holidays, along with our own cycles of living and dying, are fixed to the laws of nature. For all our swelling and ebbing waves of human civilization, we are still bound to a continual primal struggle of adaptive survivalism. More to the point, here on earth, all we get is a fleeting awareness of each other before our spirits are swept into the next experience like grains of sand, scattering ever onward.

Of Myths and Maths

Old World magick is rooted in the comfort we feel when we evoke our original human habits together. Myth is a primitive technology that unites us in learning and living together. Pagan cultural codes hide our universal mathematic mysteries in plain sight with instinctive ritualistic formulae and with sacred tools, including the domestic broom. A thing of enchantment, the broom is still used in magick as a weapon that

A thing of enchantment, the broom is still used in magick as a weapon that removes malignancy from any space and helps create a rampart of protection.

removes malignancy from any space and helps create a rampart of protection. Sacred spaces can be swept with a broom and/or surrounded by a circle of overlapping brooms to sanctify rituals or contain spirits. In very deed, the hidden earth-based wisdom of the occult is bound up today, just as ever it was, in the subtle mystery of the broom.

For many besom weavers, the tool is a perfect symbol of sacred geometry and planetary mathematics, such as those ideas explored by pagan philosopher Pythagoras. Brooms employ over/under weaving patterns that celebrate the binary laws of nature. Handcrafted brooms, when magically woven, are fixed with regional plaiting designs and patterns that use lucky numbers such as 3, 5, 7, and 9 to set a spiral, a circular, or a linear weaving order. These sacred numbers appear frequently in nature and are related to the fertility of the monthly counting cycles. These same lunar cycles are prized in astrology as indicators for routines of agricultural planning, sowing, pruning, and harvesting.

Even the sweep of the broom has a lulling sound and a spiritual power that elevates and cleanses surfaces alongside our mind, body, and spirit. As a ritual tool, the symbolic affixing of the stave, or broom rod, both mathematically and spiritually relates the besom to the sacred and procreative acts; the rod represents masculine power and the bristles represent the exotic and earthly feminine. Pagans of all types celebrate and observe this union of energies seasonally in agricultural cycles of birth, life, death, and rebirth. Every gardener knows that harnessing the fertility of the earth is all in our seasonal timing. So often it is our daily chores, like sweeping, that can have an uncanny way of revealing to us the subtle timing of our environment. For me, this symbolic wisdom elevates the broom into an elegant and unassuming emblem of the natural patterns of fertility. We achieve our higher goals with greater intention when we dance in unison and sweep the circle with the rhythms of the earth in mind.

Enchanted Sticks-in-the-Mud and the Spirits That Cleave to Them

Earth-based allegories often feature glamorous woodland creatures as well as everyday helpful spirits. The myths about these beings, based in humankind's primitive folklore, help foster in us a psychologically and spiritually positive sense of seasonal luck that is ruled by natural energetic law. Myths about domestic spirits teach us about social accountability and lend integrity to concepts of hard work and domestic labor. Domestic magick, with its many lucky numbers, spirits, folk tales, and tools, has long been designed to shift our consciousness out of the doldrums of regular labor routines and into something a little more meaningful. Sharing our everyday household work with family and coven is one way that we improve our karma together through dedicated service and social camaraderie.

In the book *The Brownies Around the World*, author Palmer Cox and his Victorian Scottish highland brownies encourage a socialist work ethic and a disengagement from ideas of overachievement or incentive beyond our own sense of personal excellence. This, and the value of patience, is exemplified in the saying "Reward oftimes is slow to fall to those who earned it best of all."

Of Magick and Mundanity

With a brownie's love of brooms in mind, the following domestic supply list and ritual is one of the many ways that we can strive to maintain cleanliness with great zeal and respect for all of the spirits living alongside us. We are merely the guardians of the earth and her creatures for this moment in time, so we must do our part to positively affect our environment while we can. For me, part of maintaining the spiritual environment of a Pagan temple is by ensuring physical and spiritual habits of cleanliness that benefit the greater community. Cleanliness is essential when providing a hospitable place of refuge for spiritual visitors and beloved guests. It is an honor to help indiscriminately process the many prayers and spells that others cast on our shared property, as we willfully open it to the general public as sacred land. This work is much more achievable when a relatively clean environment is upheld on the mundane and metaphysical levels alike.

I've yet to meet a parent who doesn't feel the same sense of responsibility for the prayers and spells of the family, cast as they should be, all about the home. Perhaps this is why adding the magick of brownies, faeries, sprites, and gnomes to communal household chores can make our active work so much more spiritually fulfilling and imaginative. Both chores and brownies teach us shared group success through maintaining consistent household integrity.

How to Stock a Broom Cupboard

These days there are all manner of cleaning robots that can zoom around the house, expending rechargeable energy with wild abandon. Ironically, few models manage to do any actual cleaning. This is, of course, because these machines are attempting to perform tasks that require the truly sacred mindfulness and intentionality of human precision. We exist in an age of immensely evolved technology, yet it still takes our mundane human tricks and frequent applications of ye olde elbow grease to successfully accomplish most domestic jobs!

One modern benefit of having so many household cleaning tools at our disposal is that there is now a decreased risk of cross-contamination from different surfaces. Contaminants on floors, counters, fixtures, toilets, and tchotchkes don't need to intermingle! Improving our conditions ensures longer and healthier lives, not to mention a more balanced energetic mode of being.

Regular cleaning prevents the spread of harmful bacteria and helps us feel spiritually safe. Peace in the home is peace in the heart. Using a few more tools can minimize labor and reduce the repetitive recleaning that becomes necessary when we merely spread filth instead of clearing it out. A broom for each job abates stagnant or negative vibes from the ceiling to the floor, finally allowing us to sweep it all out the back door for esoteric effect.

Top-Down Cleaning: The Microcosmic Zones of Life and the Flagella Among You

A time-honored top-down method, using three cleaning levels to every room, assigns to each zone a set of tools designed specifically for that purpose. These three zones are the upper level, waist level, and floor level.

Upper Level

By beginning your household cleaning with those high ceiling spots, especially in entryways, you can ensure that any and all debris will be collected as you work your way toward the floor. Stagnant debris attracts stagnant energy. Any lingering spirits in your home can be easily swept out open doors or windows, and dust bunnies can only be truly appreciated in their great numbers when they are wrangled with the proper broom and corralled into the dustbin with vim and vigor. I particularly love old cobweb brooms, with their long straw bristles and woven binding. I think these brooms are just as effective at clearing someone's mental blockages as they are at keeping the corners of the home free of cobwebs. I love the magick inherent in both

> **By beginning your household cleaning with those high ceiling spots, especially in entryways, you can ensure that any and all debris will be collected as you work your way toward the floor. Stagnant debris attracts stagnant energy. Any lingering spirits in your home can be easily swept out open doors or windows.**

uses of this broom because, as an artist, I'm always fighting stagnation and creative blockages when they arise. Perhaps to an atheist I'm just brandishing an outdated broom about the house, but to an animist I'm cleaning the house, both physically and energetically, while also cleansing my mind. Regardless of the broom or tool utilized, the action of top-down sweeping in and of itself is a dance of imagination and focus, bound to the muses and our instinctive creative impulse to make work more fun.

Waist Level

Waist-level cleaning employs all manner of spritely dusters, from feather wands to hearth brooms. Specific utility brushes and tightly bristled soft grass brooms are wonderful for cleaning the bric-a-brac and artwork displayed throughout one's home. Many cleaners, like the feather duster, make use of a naturally occurring static charge to cause dust to cling to its surface. Sweeping fuzzy bunnies out of these dust collectors is the best way to reduce environmental allergens, pet dander, and stagnant energies throughout the home. I find that gorgeous peacock plumage dusters also give a protective panache where modern microfibers fall short.

Floor Level

At the floor level, brownies and gnomes can guide our upright heavy-duty and angular brooms. These tools can reach deeply into household nooks and crannies, helping us clean down to the last crumb. To aid this process, one can employ a simple dustpan and hand broom, making quick work of the piles that accumulate when sweeping with a standard broom. Carpet brooms and rug beaters help take the dirt back outside when area rugs begin to look more like the local ecosystem than the inside world. Finally, a straw broom is favored for steps and porches. This traditional symbol of rural magick is a common feature and is a welcome sign proudly displayed resting at the entrance of many Pagan homes to invite luck, love, and kindred souls to gather there.

To Create a Magick Broom Cupboard

Now it's time to create your own magick broom cupboard.

Supplies

First assemble the following items:

- Double-sided tape
- Incense charcoal patty and a safe burner
- Frankincense resin
- Nontoxic permanent markers

- 12 inches of black thread

- Ocean water for anointing (or create your own with sea salt)

- Tea tree (melaleuca) pure essential oil for anointing

Next, acquire the following seven Tarot cards from a used copy of your favorite deck. Affix a small piece of double-sided tape to the back of each card and carefully set them aside in this order:

1. The World: XXI

2. The Tower: XVI

3. The Empress: III

4. The Sun: XIX

5. The Wheel of Fortune: X

6. The Magician: I

7. The High Priestess: II

Now gather all of your brooms and cleaning supplies, including but not limited to the following:

- Ritual besom

- Upright heavy-duty broom

- Angled kitchen broom

- Dustpan and hand broom

- Straw porch and stair broom

- Hearth broom

- Cobweb broom

- Rags and dusters

- Wool mops and dusters

- Microfiber mop

- Mopping bucket

PROCEDURE

1. Empty out your broom closet or broom cupboard to prepare for your magickal work.

2. Banish dust bunnies to start the ritual. Ward off all boggarts, grindylows, and other undesirables by ringing bells throughout the empty cupboard and stating affirmations of purpose. Goal-oriented affirmations or mantras are fun when seasonally cleaning. "Our clean home is inviting" is a good example. Really, anything said with true meaning and intent will do. I've used everything from the casual Black Knight's banter "None shall pass" to the optimist's vigorous declaration "By my Will, so mote it be."

3. Clean and wash the empty cupboard, from ceiling to floor, using a strong all-natural antibacterial cleaner such as vinegar or Van Van.

4. Enchant and personalize each cleaning tool. Conjure your intentions by drawing gnomes, brownies, planetary symbols, and images from the various Tarot cards selected. Draw your wishes, protection prayers, and sigils of power onto the tools with permanent markers. Don't forget to add stickers or images of faeries and little elves on the tools as well as the inner walls of your broom cupboard! Hang forest posters or mystical pictures close to the floor to create a sense of wonderland within.

5. Anoint each cleaning tool with a dab of tea tree oil and ocean water.

6. Organize all your brooms, mops, buckets, and cleaners into the broom cupboard in a manner that feels energetically appealing and orderly.

7. Asperge the cupboard with ocean water and broadcast sea salt to remove any last speck of negativity.

8. Cast a sacred rampart by stating:

Cleanliness I cast, my willful intent evoked here! Behold a treasure trove of health, productivity, and purification. I draw a field against stagnation and disease; I call forth the light of life to banish the malignant energies of rot and decay. Spirits of the earth, come now to this place! Preserve and maintain domestic order within and all around the space that I conjure before thee.

9. Summon the elements in the manner to which you are accustomed. Call to each element in nature and ask them to reinforce this rampart of protection in their own unique way.

10. Ignite the charcoal and burn the frankincense. As you do so, express your reasons for inviting better cleaning habits into your routine. Call upon gnomes, sprites, faeries, brownies, and helpful spirits to inspire and motivate positive changes within you. Ask them to help you shoulder the workload to make jobs easier with their help. In exchange, leave them offerings of ale, honey, milk, mushrooms, and doll house furniture or natural objects of microscopic interest. Ensure that you return in a week's time to clean and replace any perishable offerings.

11. Dedicate the cupboard with Tarot cards by affixing the cards securely to each directional surface in the cupboard. Place them in the following order and speak each provided prayer aloud:

1. The World: XXI (Saturn)—Hang by a black thread from the ceiling:
Here, where I find myself.

2. The Tower: XVI (Mars)—North wall:
That which I must destroy to find peace.

3. The Empress: III (Venus)—East wall:
Such sweet wishes shall nourish me.

4. The Sun: XIX (Sol)—South wall:
Radiant is that which motivates me.

5. The Wheel of Fortune: X (Jupiter)—West wall:
By this thriving luck will all be fulfilled.

6. The Magician: I (Mercury)—Ceiling:
With this magick my uniformity and will be done.

7. The High Priestess: II (Moon)—Floor:
For my emotions are the intelligence that prevails.

12. Schedule a day of the week to uphold your magickal intent by cleaning the house and working to fulfill healthy personal goals.

13. Offer thanks and gratitude to the spirits, and allow the incense to fully burn out. Give thanks in the way to which you are accustomed and depart in peace.

Blessed be the sacred broom cupboard!

Sources

Blake, Deborah. *The Witch's Broom: The Craft, Lore & Magick of Broomsticks.* Woodbury, MN: Llewellyn, 2014.

Cox, Palmer. *The Brownies Around the World.* 1894. Reprint, London: Forgotten Books, 2012.

To Learn More

CedarRoot Folk School, http://cedarrootfolkschool.org

Handmade Ozark Brooms, www.angelfire.com/ar/ozarkbrooms/BROOM .html

Estha McNevin (Missoula, MT) *is a Priestess and ceremonial oracle of Opus Aima Obscuræ, a nonprofit Pagan temple haus. She has served the Pagan community since 2003 as an Eastern Hellenistic officiate, lecturer, freelance author, artist, and poet. Estha studies and teaches courses on ancient and modern Pagan history. She offers classes on multicultural metaphysical theory, ritual technique, international cuisine, organic gardening, herbal craft, alchemy, and occult symbolism. In addition to hosting public rituals for the sabbats, Estha organizes annual philanthropic fundraisers, full moon spellcrafting ceremonies, and women's divination rituals for each dark moon. To learn more, please explore www.facebook.com/opusaimaobscurae.*

Illustrator: Bri Hermanson

Vox Magicae: Using the Voice as a Magical Tool

Devin Hunter

The most powerful acts of magic that I have witnessed have been performed in song or chant. Some of these have been while leading large groups of people at a convention during a workshop or ritual, but I have also seen incredibly deep magic performed by a witch at her spindle as she sang to the newly spun fibers and invoked the power of her gods. Whether it's the moans of a birthing mother, the decree of a master magician, or the sound of a children's choir, no one can argue that the voice is a magical tool capable of projecting our innermost will.

As a professionally trained vocalist, I know well the hidden possibilities waiting to be unlocked by the voice. When I was growing up, every time I sang I was having a spiritual experience. The probability of there being a connection between the occult and music theory in my world was more of an inevitability. I was raised singing in church, so I knew the voice could be used as a tool of devotion, but it wasn't until I sat down with a piano and a few willing guinea pigs that I was able to shed some light on the subject.

In my witchcraft community, every act of great devotion, every ritual that requires an immense amount of energy, and every working that touches the soul must include an element of vocal magic, or, as we call it, the *Vox Magicae*. As opposed to the Ephesian letters known as the *Voces Magicae*, which focus specifically on words, Vox Magicae is the study of the voice in magic and how we use it. Vox Magicae means

"Voice of Magic" in Latin, and has several major points of interest. Let's look at two of them: the power of words and their articulation, and the resonance of the soul and how to either amplify or adjust it when needed.

The Power of Words

Words have power, and how we say them or sing them shapes the way that power manifests. To ensure that the vocal component of your magic is shaping that energy properly and efficiently, you have to become familiar with the concept of diction and how it relates to your spells. Later, when working with the powers of the voice, placing an importance on diction can help take your magic to the next level.

> **Words have power, and how we say them or sing them shapes the way that power manifests. To ensure that the vocal component of your magic is shaping that energy properly and efficiently, you have to become familiar with the concept of diction and how it relates to your spells.**

Diction is the way and the style in which we shape our words as we speak them. Included in this are accent and inflexion, two aspects of speech that are important to note. Unless you are a singer, your accent isn't too much of a problem. I come from southern Ohio and have a noticeable "hick" accent that I have worked hard at taming over the years. It's okay to have an accent as long as your words are spoken clearly. If the word *creek* sounds like the word *crick* when you say it, that's okay as long as you say crick with conviction and clarity. Regional accents and dialogue are an intricate part of historical witchcraft that should be embraced as long as they don't get in the way. Your inflexion, on the other hand, is the tone in your voice in which emotional information is transmitted. In witchcraft, our inflexion must possess strength, which can be provided through a steady, deeper tone. Aside from accent and inflexion, we have to make sure that we are pronouncing words fully and articulating their unique sounds completely.

Playing with Diction

Read aloud the following spell for good luck and try to fully pronounce each word. After you have read it out loud a few times and have picked up the rhythm of the words in the poetry, try to say it a few different ways. Whisper it a few times, sing it to the tune of "Baa, Baa, Black Sheep," and lastly, say it like a Shakespearean actor. Notice the way the same spell can have a completely different feeling to it when spoken with a different diction.

Good Luck Spell

White Rabbit, White Rabbit, skipping through the snow,
A streak of luck, a shot at fortune, everywhere you go.
Left foot, right foot, walking to and fro,
Picking up the luck you drop, let the blessings flow!

The Harmony of Souls

In my first book, The Witch's Book of Power, I put forth the idea that we can associate specific octaves (the space of eight steps between harmonic intervals) with different layers of the soul. In my tradition we use the Three Soul model, which describes the soul as existing in three separate parts: the primal soul, the ego soul, and the higher soul (sometimes known as the holy soul). Each of these souls has its own psychic resonance, which we call *frequency*.

The frequency of the primal soul vibrates the lowest of the three souls. In Western music theory, this frequency resonates with notes C2 (Low C) to B3. Within these two octaves, any tone played or sung by someone with a deep bass or baritone voice can have an immediate effect on the primal soul. These tones can release lower-frequency energies that attach during times of dis-ease and can be used to promote life force production in the primal soul.

The ego soul resonates with notes C4 (Middle C) to B5. Any note played within this range can activate and energize the primal soul, especially when chords are present. These tones can also be played to expand the aura, providing easier access to the internal energy systems.

The frequency of the higher self resonates the highest of the three souls and, in Western music theory, harmonizes with notes C6 (High C) to B7. Soprano voices can sing these notes, and when used in harmonic therapies these tones will cause lower frequencies to release from the energy body. In my work I have found that these notes can also (when played softly in chord progressions over long durations of time) increase psychic sensitivity.

When the three souls are aligned, meaning that we have grounded and centered our energy and called upon our divine authority, these three parts unite to create a choir of energies that we refer to as the *home frequency*, or your *Holy Fire*. Your home frequency resonates out into the universe in all directions and carries with it your magic and other forms of psychic information. If each of the three souls is resonating with a unique frequency, then when combined those individual frequencies would look something like a chord being played on a piano. The more harmonic the chord, the stronger the resonance of the home frequency and the brighter the Holy Fire.

Finding Your Harmony: A Quick Guide

Go to a piano or download one of the multiple free piano apps. Take a few moments to warm up your voice by singing your favorite song or nursery rhyme. Once you are warmed up, find C2 (Low C) on your piano and play it. Listen to the tone and then try your best to match it as you sing or "tone" the vowel *Ahh*. Play the note again and repeat the process of toning. Move from C2 to B2 on the piano, playing only natural notes (the white keys) in this way. Don't worry about being an excellent singer or having perfect pitch or even singing in the same octave; just open your mouth and sing. The purpose of this exercise is to determine which notes feel the best to you when you hear and sing them.

With this exercise we are looking for a note to evoke some sort of psychic or emotional response in us when we sing it. We also want to pay attention to the ease with which that note is sung. Again, it is okay if you aren't singing in the right octave; a person can match pitch even if they aren't singing in the same octave. This range would be difficult, if not impossible, for many higher voices to reach, so don't think in terms of the octave, think in terms of how the sound affects you. Is it difficult to get the note out of your mouth? Though the pitch doesn't have to be spot on, can you match pitch close enough when you sing? As you move through the octave, pay attention to how you respond to each note. Once you have moved through the entire octave, determine which note you resonate most with and jot it down.

Repeat this process for C4 (Middle C) to B4 and then for C6 (High C) to B6. Once you have finished, take a look at the notes you felt most in resonance with during each pass-through. Using the notes between C4 and B4, play the first two notes that you jotted down simultaneously. How do they sound when played together? Do they sound harmonic or dissonant? Now play the second and third notes. How do those sound together? Next, play the first and third notes. What do they sound like when played together?

Ideally, when we are aligned and in a place of power, all of these notes will sound harmonic when played together. In the event that you had the same note present itself multiple times, take that as a sign that this note is associated with the resonance of your home frequency. If you find that all three notes sound great together, then proceed to the next phase of the exercise. If one of the notes sounds off from the other two, you will need to either raise or lower the vibration of that note. If none of the notes sound good when played together and are full of dissonance, then I recommend adjusting them based off the highest note and then altering one of the two lower notes to reach harmony.

Ideally, when we are aligned and in a place of power, all of these notes will sound harmonic when played together.

Adjusting Your Resonance

When we need to adjust a tone because it is causing dissonance or because we wish to alter the way our frequency is transmitting, we take two things into consideration. The first is to remember that each note is associated with specific energies that we can draw from in order to adjust each frequency as needed. Each note carries with it a unique vibrational energy:

C – The home frequency, personal resonance, mental and spiritual clarity, and divine authority

D – Pride, consciousness, and projection

E – Willpower, focus, and magical inheritance

F – Sex, passion, generational healing, and physical inheritance

G – Life force, Gaia, the fighting will to survive, and the flame of Faery

A – Vitality, community, self-discipline, and manifestation

B – The second sight, spirits, and soul flight

C + C – Spiritual healing, soul recovery, karma, and sacred contracts (C + C represents the harmonic interval)

The second thing to keep in mind is that we must use the voice to help make this adjustment. To do this, we sing the note and think about what vibrational energy it is associated with by toning the note using the vowel *Ooh*. While toning, we meditate on what that energy might mean to us and why it has presented itself this way. We then adjust the tone by either going up or going down one note and then toning the vowel *Eee*. This time as we tone we allow our frequency to adjust as well and use the new tone to stimulate the desired frequency modification. Spend several minutes toning this way until you feel grounded in the new frequency.

Practice this twice a week for a few weeks as a tool for conscious energy adjustment. The more time you spend performing this, the more your mind will perceive frequency adjustment as a process of seeking harmony. Journal your findings and meditate on the thoughts, emotions, and visions you experience during this practice. Know that anything you evoke during the process of toning has surfaced for a reason, and that by diligently working through these things you can free yourself of burdensome mental and psychic energies.

· · · · · · · · · · · ·

The voice is a powerful tool that can be used to increase influence and dominion as well as to heal and empower. It can show our weaknesses to the world and it can command the heavens. Vox Magicae is the magic of consciously turning the voice into a deliberate magical tool and using that tool to propel our desire forward. Sometimes that involves deeply personal works and other times it involves the art of using the voice to fascinate the unsuspecting. As with every practice, the ethical implications are yours to determine. You must choose the best road for yourself. However you decide to work the Vox Magicae, breathe deep and speak with power of the God within.

Devin Hunter (San Francisco Bay Area) is a bestselling author who holds initiations in multiple spiritual, occult, and esoteric traditions and is the founder of his own tradition, Sacred Fires, and co-founder of its offshoot community, Black Rose Witchcraft. His podcast, The Modern Witch, has helped thousands of people from all over the world empower themselves and discover their psychic and magical abilities. Devin is the co-owner of the Mystic Dream, a metaphysical store in Walnut Creek, CA, where he offers professional services as a medium and occultist.

Illustrator: Rik Olson

The Lunar Calendar

September 2018 to December 2019

SEPTEMBER

S	M	T	W	T	F	S
						1
2	3	4	5	6	7	8
9	10	11	12	13	14	15
16	17	18	19	20	21	22
23	24	25	26	27	28	29
30						

OCTOBER

S	M	T	W	T	F	S
	1	2	3	4	5	6
7	8	9	10	11	12	13
14	15	16	17	18	19	20
21	22	23	24	25	26	27
28	29	30	31			

NOVEMBER

S	M	T	W	T	F	S
				1	2	3
4	5	6	7	8	9	10
11	12	13	14	15	16	17
18	19	20	21	22	23	24
25	26	27	28	29	30	

DECEMBER

S	M	T	W	T	F	S
						1
2	3	4	5	6	7	8
9	10	11	12	13	14	15
16	17	18	19	20	21	22
23	24	25	26	27	28	29
30	31					

2019

JANUARY

S	M	T	W	T	F	S
		1	2	3	4	5
6	7	8	9	10	11	12
13	14	15	16	17	18	19
20	21	22	23	24	25	26
27	28	29	30	31		

FEBRUARY

S	M	T	W	T	F	S
					1	2
3	4	5	6	7	8	9
10	11	12	13	14	15	16
17	18	19	20	21	22	23
24	25	26	27	28		

MARCH

S	M	T	W	T	F	S
					1	2
3	4	5	6	7	8	9
10	11	12	13	14	15	16
17	18	19	20	21	22	23
24	25	26	27	28	29	30
31						

APRIL

S	M	T	W	T	F	S
	1	2	3	4	5	6
7	8	9	10	11	12	13
14	15	16	17	18	19	20
21	22	23	24	25	26	27
28	29	30				

MAY

S	M	T	W	T	F	S
			1	2	3	4
5	6	7	8	9	10	11
12	13	14	15	16	17	18
19	20	21	22	23	24	25
26	27	28	29	30	31	

JUNE

S	M	T	W	T	F	S
						1
2	3	4	5	6	7	8
9	10	11	12	13	14	15
16	17	18	19	20	21	22
23	24	25	26	27	28	29
30						

JULY

S	M	T	W	T	F	S
	1	2	3	4	5	6
7	8	9	10	11	12	13
14	15	16	17	18	19	20
21	22	23	24	25	26	27
28	29	30	31			

AUGUST

S	M	T	W	T	F	S
				1	2	3
4	5	6	7	8	9	10
11	12	13	14	15	16	17
18	19	20	21	22	23	24
25	26	27	28	29	30	31

SEPTEMBER

S	M	T	W	T	F	S
1	2	3	4	5	6	7
8	9	10	11	12	13	14
15	16	17	18	19	20	21
22	23	24	25	26	27	28
29	30					

OCTOBER

S	M	T	W	T	F	S
		1	2	3	4	5
6	7	8	9	10	11	12
13	14	15	16	17	18	19
20	21	22	23	24	25	26
27	28	29	30	31		

NOVEMBER

S	M	T	W	T	F	S
					1	2
3	4	5	6	7	8	9
10	11	12	13	14	15	16
17	18	19	20	21	22	23
24	25	26	27	28	29	30

DECEMBER

S	M	T	W	T	F	S
1	2	3	4	5	6	7
8	9	10	11	12	13	14
15	16	17	18	19	20	21
22	23	24	25	26	27	28
29	30	31				

SEPTEMBER 2018

SU	M	T	W
26	**27**	**28**	**29**
2 3rd ♉ ☽ v/c 1:56 am ☽ → ♊ 4:02 am 4th Quarter 10:37 pm ◐	**3** 4th ♊ *Labor Day*	**4** 4th ♊ ☽ v/c 2:37 am ☽ → ♋ 8:03 am	**5** 4th ♋
9 4th ♍ New Moon 2:01 pm ● *New Moon*	**10** 1st ♍ ☽ v/c 11:12 am ☽ → ♎ 11:20 am	**11** 1st ♎ ☽ v/c 6:58 pm	**12** 1st ♎ ☽ → ♏ 2:15 pm
16 1st ♐ ☽ v/c 7:15 pm 2nd Quarter 7:15 pm ◑	**17** 2nd ♐ ☽ → ♑ 7:07 am	**18** 2nd ♑	**19** 2nd ♑ ☽ v/c 1:10 pm ☽ → ♒ 7:52 pm
23 2nd ♓	**24** 2nd ♓ ☽ v/c 1:26 am ☽ → ♈ 7:04 am Full Moon 10:52 pm ○ *Harvest Moon*	**25** 3rd ♈	**26** 3rd ♈ ☽ v/c 6:28 am
30 3rd ♊ ☽ v/c 11:38 am	**1**	**2**	**3**

Eastern Daylight Time (EDT)

ZODIAC SIGNS

♈ Aries	♌ Leo	♐ Sagittarius
♉ Taurus	♍ Virgo	♑ Capricorn
♊ Gemini	♎ Libra	♒ Aquarius
♋ Cancer	♏ Scorpio	♓ Pisces

PLANETS

☉ Sun	♃ Jupiter
☽ Moon	♄ Saturn
☿ Mercury	♅ Uranus
♀ Venus	♆ Neptune
♂ Mars	♇ Pluto

SEPTEMBER 2018

TH	F	SA	NOTES
30	31	3rd ♉ 1	
4th ⊗ 6 ☽ v/c 8:43 am ☽ → ♌ 9:54 am	4th ♌ 7	4th ♌ 8 ☽ v/c 9:31 am ☽ → ♍ 10:29 am	
1st ♏ 13	1st ♏ 14 ☽ v/c 4:54 am ☽ → ♐ 8:45 pm	1st ♐ 15	
2nd ≈ 20	2nd ≈ 21 ☽ v/c 1:13 pm	2nd ≈ 22 ☽ → ♓ 8:27 am ☉ → ♎ 9:54 pm *Mabon* *Sun enters Libra* *Fall Equinox*	
3rd ♈ 27 ☽ → ♉ 3:16 am	3rd ♉ 28 ☽ v/c 6:36 pm	3rd ♉ 29 ☽ → ♊ 9:26 am	
4	5	6	

ASPECTS & MOON PHASES

☌ Conjunction	0°	● New Moon	(1st Quarter)
✳ Sextile	60°	◐ Waxing Moon	(2nd Quarter)
□ Square	90°	○ Full Moon	(3rd Quarter)
△ Trine	120°	◑ Waning Moon	(4th Quarter)
⊼ Quincunx	150°		
☍ Opposition	180°		

OCTOBER 2018

SU	M	T	W
30	1 — 3rd ♊ ☽ → ♋ 2:00 pm	3rd ♋ 4th Quarter 5:45 am ◐	3 — 4th ♋ ☽ v/c 4:33 am ☽ → ♌ 5:12 pm
7 — 4th ♍ ☽ v/c 10:03 am ☽ → ♎ 9:10 pm	8 — 4th ♎ New Moon 11:47 pm ● *New Moon*	9 — 1st ♎ ☽ v/c 4:50 am	10 — 1ot ♎ ☽ → ♏ 12:09 am
14 — 1st ♐ ☽ → ♑ 3:17 pm	15 — 1st ♑	16 — 1st ♑ 2nd Quarter 2:02 pm ☽ v/c 5:49 pm ◑	17 — 2nd ♑ ☽ → ♒ 3:36 am
21 — 2nd ♓ ☽ v/c 7:47 pm	22 — 2nd ♓ ☽ → ♈ 2:58 am	23 — 2nd ♈ ☉ → ♏ 7:22 am ☽ v/c 2:18 pm *Sun enters Scorpio*	24 — 2nd ♈ ☽ → ♉ 10:33 am Full Moon 12:45 pm ○ *Blood Moon*
28 — 3rd ♊ ☽ v/c 12:37 am ☽ → ♋ 7:27 am	29 — 3rd ♋	30 — 3rd ♋ ☽ v/c 10:31 pm ☽ → ♌ 10:42 pm *Samhain* *Halloween*	31 — 3rd ♌ 4th Quarter 12:40 pm ◐
4	5	6	7

Eastern Daylight Time (EDT)

ZODIAC SIGNS

♈ Aries	♌ Leo
♉ Taurus	♍ Virgo
♊ Gemini	♎ Libra
♋ Cancer	♏ Scorpio

♐ Sagittarius	
♑ Capricorn	
♒ Aquarius	
♓ Pisces	

PLANETS

☉ Sun	♃ Jupiter
☽ Moon	♄ Saturn
☿ Mercury	♅ Uranus
♀ Venus	♆ Neptune
♂ Mars	♇ Pluto

OCTOBER 2018

TH	F	SA	NOTES
4th ♌ **4**	4th ♌ **5** ☽ v/c 7:34 am ♀ ℞ 3:04 pm ☽ → ♍ 7:19 pm *Venus retrograde*	4th ♍ **6**	
1st ♏ **11** ☽ v/c 7:12 pm	1st ♏ **12** ☽ → ♐ 5:53 am	1st ♐ **13** ☽ v/c 8:58 pm	
2nd ♒ **18**	2nd ♒ **19** ☽ v/c 8:27 am ☽ → ♓ 4:20 pm	2nd ♓ **20**	
3rd ♉ **25**	3rd ♉ **26** ☽ v/c 10:49 am ☽ → ♊ 3:41 pm	3rd ♊ **27**	
1	**2**	**3**	
8	**9**	**10**	

ASPECTS & MOON PHASES

☌ Conjunction	0°	● New Moon	(1st Quarter)
⚹ Sextile	60°	◑ Waxing Moon	(2nd Quarter)
☐ Square	90°	○ Full Moon	(3rd Quarter)
△ Trine	120°	◐ Waning Moon	(4th Quarter)
⚻ Quincunx	150°		
☍ Opposition	180°		

NOVEMBER 2018

SU	M	T	W
28	29	30	31
4 4th ♍ ☽ v/c 2:26 am ☽ → ♎ 4:01 am *Daylight Saving Time ends at 2:00 am*	**5** 4th ♎	**6** 4th ♎ ☽ v/c 3:19 am ☽ → ♏ 8:02 am *Election Day (general)*	**31** 4th ♏ New Moon 11:02 am ● New Moon
11 1st ♑	**12** 1st ♑	**13** 1st ♑ ☽ v/c 10:13 am ☽ → ♒ 10:45 am	**14** 1st ♒
18 2nd ♓ ☽ v/c 3:04 am ☽ → ♈ 10:56 am	**19** 2nd ♈	**20** 2nd ♈ ☽ v/c 5:46 pm ☽ → ♉ 6:43 pm	**21** 2nd ♉
25 3rd ♊ ☽ v/c 12:31 am ☽ → ♋ 1:38 am	**26** 3rd ♋	**27** 3rd ♋ ☽ v/c 2:22 am ☽ → ♌ 3:35 am	**28** 3rd ♌
2	3	4	5

Eastern Daylight Time (EDT) becomes Eastern Standard Time (EST) November 4

ZODIAC SIGNS

♈ Aries	♌ Leo	♐ Sagittarius
♉ Taurus	♍ Virgo	♑ Capricorn
♊ Gemini	♎ Libra	♒ Aquarius
♋ Cancer	♏ Scorpio	♓ Pisces

PLANETS

☉ Sun	♃ Jupiter
☽ Moon	♄ Saturn
☿ Mercury	♅ Uranus
♀ Venus	♆ Neptune
♂ Mars	♇ Pluto

NOVEMBER 2018

TH	F	SA	NOTES
4th ♌ **1**	4th ♌ **2** ☽ v/c 12:32 am ☽ → ♍ 1:48 am	4th ♍ **3**	
1st ♏ **8** ☽ v/c 5:42 am ☽ → ♐ 1:59 pm	1st ♐ **9**	1st ♐ **10** ☽ v/c 10:35 pm ☽ → ♑ 10:55 pm	
1st ♒ ◑ **16** 2nd Quarter 9:54 am ☽ v/c 10:58 pm ☽ → ♓ 11:41 pm	2nd ♓ **16** ♀ D 5:51 am ☿ ℞ 8:33 pm *Venus direct* *Mercury retrograde*	2nd ♓ **17**	
2nd ♉ **22** ☉ → ♐ 4:01 am ☽ v/c 4:59 am ☽ → ♊ 11:10 pm *Thanksgiving Day* *Sun enters Sagittarius*	2nd ♊ ○ **23** Full Moon 12:39 am *Mourning Moon*	3rd ♊ **24**	
3rd ♌ ◑ **29** ☽ v/c 4:47 am ☽ → ♍ 6:08 pm 4th Quarter 7:19 pm	4th ♍ **30**	*1*	
6	*7*	*8*	

ASPECTS & MOON PHASES

☌ Conjunction	0°	● New Moon	(1st Quarter)
⚹ Sextile	60°	◑ Waxing Moon	(2nd Quarter)
▢ Square	90°	○ Full Moon	(3rd Quarter)
△ Trine	120°	◐ Waning Moon	(4th Quarter)
⚻ Quincunx	150°		
☍ Opposition	180°		

DECEMBER 2018

SU	M	T	W
25	26	27	28
4th ♎︎ 2	4th ♎︎ 3 ☽ v/c 1:16 pm ☽ → ♏︎ 2:55 pm	4th ♏︎ 4	4th ♏︎ 5 ☽ v/c 4:53 pm ☽ → ♐︎ 9:49 pm
1st ♑︎ 9	1st ♑︎ 10 ☽ v/c 4:27 pm ☽ → ♒︎ 6:39 pm	1st ♒︎ 11	1st ♒︎ 12
2nd ♈︎ 16	2nd ♈︎ 17	2nd ♈︎ 18 ☽ v/c 2:21 am ☽ → ♉︎ 4:37 am	2nd ♉︎ 19 ☽ v/c 7:42 pm
3rd ⊗ 23	3rd ⊗ 24 ☽ v/c 9:50 am ☽ → ♌︎ 11:59 am *Christmas Eve*	3rd ♌︎ 25 *Christmas Day*	3rd ♌︎ 26 ☽ v/c 10:37 am ☽ → ♍︎ 12:50 pm
4th ♎︎ 30 ☽ v/c 5:53 pm ☽ → ♏︎ 8:23 pm	4th ♏︎ 31 *New Year's Eve*	1	2

Eastern Standard Time (EST)

ZODIAC SIGNS

♈︎ Aries	♌︎ Leo	♐︎ Sagittarius
♉︎ Taurus	♍︎ Virgo	♑︎ Capricorn
♊︎ Gemini	♎︎ Libra	♒︎ Aquarius
♋︎ Cancer	♏︎ Scorpio	♓︎ Pisces

PLANETS

☉ Sun	♃ Jupiter
☽ Moon	♄ Saturn
☿ Mercury	♅ Uranus
♀ Venus	♆ Neptune
♂ Mars	♇ Pluto

DECEMBER 2018

TH	F	SA	NOTES
29	30	**1** 4th ♍ ☽ v/c 9:34 am ☽ → ♎ 9:49 am	
6 4th ♐ ☿ D 4:22 pm *Mercury direct*	**New Moon** ● 4th ♐ New Moon 2:20 am *New Moon*	**8** 1st ♐ ☽ v/c 5:00 am ☽ → ♑ 7:01 am	
13 1st ♒ ☽ v/c 5:20 am ☽ → ♓ 7:40 am	**14** 1st ♓	**●** 1st ♓ ☽ v/c 6:49 am 2nd Quarter 6:49 am ☽ → ♈ 7:44 pm	
20 2nd ♉ ☽ → ♊ 9:34 am	**21** 2nd ♊ ☉ → ♑ 5:23 pm *Yule* *Sun enters Capricorn* *Winter Solstice*	**○** 2nd ♊ ☽ v/c 9:21 am ☽ → ♋ 11:28 am Full Moon 12:49 pm *Long Nights Moon*	
27 3rd ♍	**28** 3rd ♍ ☽ v/c 11:27 am ☽ → ♎ 3:23 pm	**●** 3rd ♎ 4th Quarter 4:34 am	
3	4	5	

ASPECTS & MOON PHASES

☌ Conjunction	0°	● New Moon	(1st Quarter)
✶ Sextile	60°	◑ Waxing Moon	(2nd Quarter)
☐ Square	90°	○ Full Moon	(3rd Quarter)
△ Trine	120°	◑ Waning Moon	(4th Quarter)
⚻ Quincunx	150°		
☍ Opposition	180°		

JANUARY 2019

SU	M	T	W
30	31	4th ♏ ☽ v/c 5:26 pm **1** New Year's Day	4th ♏ **2** ☽ → ♐ 3:58 am
1st ♑ **6**	1st ♑ **7** ☽ v/c 1:20 am ☽ → ♒ 1:46 am	1st ♒ **8**	1st ♒ **9** ☽ v/c 11:53 am ☽ → ♓ 2:44 pm
1st ♈ **13**	1st ♈ **14** ◐ 2nd Quarter 1:46 am ☽ v/c 10:56 am ☽ → ♉ 1:31 pm	2nd ♉ **15**	2nd ♉ **16** ☽ v/c 1:34 pm ☽ → ♊ 8:00 pm
2nd ♋ **20** ☉ → ♒ 4:00 am ☽ v/c 8:50 pm ☽ → ♌ 10:54 pm Sun enters Aquarius	2nd ♌ **21** ○ Full Moon 12:16 am Martin Luther King Jr. Day Cold Moon Lunar Eclipse	3rd ♌ **22** ☽ v/c 8:19 pm ☽ → ♍ 10:22 pm	3rd ♍ **23**
3rd ♎ **27** ☽ v/c 12:21 am ☽ → ♏ 2:31 am 4th Quarter 4:10 pm	4th ♏ **28** ◑ ☽ v/c 5:39 pm	4th ♏ **29** ☽ → ♐ 9:33 am	4th ♐ **30**
3	4	5	6

Eastern Standard Time (EST)

ZODIAC SIGNS

♈ Aries	♌ Leo
♉ Taurus	♍ Virgo
♊ Gemini	♎ Libra
♋ Cancer	♏ Scorpio

♐ Sagittarius	
♑ Capricorn	
♒ Aquarius	
♓ Pisces	

PLANETS

☉ Sun	♃ Jupiter
☽ Moon	♄ Saturn
☿ Mercury	♅ Uranus
♀ Venus	♆ Neptune
♂ Mars	♇ Pluto

JANUARY 2019

TH	F	SA	NOTES
4th ♐ **3**	4th ♐ **4** ☽ v/c 12:41 pm ☽ → ♑ 1:55 pm	4th ♑ ● New Moon 8:28 pm *New Moon* *Solar Eclipse*	
1st ♓ **10**	1st ♓ **11** ☽ v/c 9:25 am	1st ♓ **12** ☽ → ♈ 3:18 am	
2nd ♊ **17**	2nd ♊ **18** ☽ v/c 8:32 pm ☽ → ♋ 10:44 pm	2nd ♋ **19**	
3rd ♍ **24** ☽ v/c 8:50 am ☽ → ♎ 11:02 pm	3rd ♎ **25**	3rd ♎ **26**	
4th ♐ **31** ☽ v/c 5:33 pm ☽ → ♑ 7:47 pm	**1**	**2**	
7	**8**	**9**	

FEBRUARY 2019

SU	M	T	W
27	28	29	30
3 4th ♑ ☽ v/c 5:53 am ☽ → ♒ 8:03 am	**4** 4th ♒ New Moon 4:04 pm ● *New Moon*	**5** 1st ♒ ☽ v/c 6:59 pm ☽ → ♓ 9:02 pm	**6** 1st ♓
10 1st ♈ ☽ v/c 6:48 pm ☽ → ♉ 8:28 pm	**11** 1st ♉	**12** 1st ♉ ◐ ☽ v/c 5:26 pm 2nd Quarter 5:26 pm	**13** 2nd ♉ ☽ → ♊ 4:32 am s
17 2nd ♋ ☽ v/c 9:17 am ☽ → ♌ 10:21 am	**18** 2nd ♌ ☉ → ♓ 6:04 pm *Sun enters Pisces* *Presidents' Day*	**19** 2nd ♌ ○ ☽ v/c 8:51 am ☽ → ♍ 9:47 am Full Moon 10:54 am *Quickening Moon*	**20** 3rd ♍ ☽ v/c 8:52 pm
24 3rd ♏	**25** 3rd ♏ ☽ v/c 7:14 am ☽ → ♐ 4:19 pm	**26** 3rd ♐ ◐ 4th Quarter 6:28 am	**27** 4th ♐
3	4	5	6

Eastern Standard Time (EST)

ZODIAC SIGNS

♈ Aries	♌ Leo	♐ Sagittarius
♉ Taurus	♍ Virgo	♑ Capricorn
♊ Gemini	♎ Libra	♒ Aquarius
♋ Cancer	♏ Scorpio	♓ Pisces

PLANETS

☉ Sun	♃ Jupiter
☽ Moon	♄ Saturn
☿ Mercury	♅ Uranus
♀ Venus	♆ Neptune
♂ Mars	♇ Pluto

TH	F	SA	NOTES
31	**1** 4th ♑	**2** 4th ♑ *Imbolc* *Groundhog Day*	
7 1st ♓ ☽ v/c 5:14 pm	**8** 1st ♓ ☽ → ♈ 9:34 am	**9** 1st ♈	
14 2nd ♊ *Valentine's Day*	**15** 2nd ♊ ☽ v/c 7:48 am ☽ → ♋ 9:03 am	**16** 2nd ♋	
21 3rd ♍ ☽ → ♎ 9:17 am	**22** 3rd ♎	**23** 3rd ♎ ☽ v/c 10:11 am ☽ → ♏ 10:56 am	
28 4th ♐ ☽ v/c 1:17 am ☽ → ♑ 1:48 am	1	2	
7	8	9	

ASPECTS & MOON PHASES

☌ Conjunction	0°	● New Moon	(1st Quarter)
✶ Sextile	60°	◐ Waxing Moon	(2nd Quarter)
□ Square	90°	○ Full Moon	(3rd Quarter)
△ Trine	120°	◑ Waning Moon	(4th Quarter)
⊼ Quincunx	150°		
☍ Opposition	180°		

MARCH 2019

SU	M	T	W
24	**25**	**26**	**27**
3 4th ≈	**4** 4th ≈	**5** 4th ≈ ☽ v/c 3:05 am ☽ → ♓ 3:11 am ☿℞ 1:19 pm *Mercury retrograde*	**27 ●** 4th ♓ New Moon 11:04 am *New Moon*
10 1st ♈ ☽ → ♉ 3:10 am *Daylight Saving Time* *begins at 2:00 am*	**11** 1st ♉	**12** 1st ♉ ☽ v/c 5:31 am ☽ → ♊ 11:48 am	**13** 1st ♊
17 2nd ♌ *St. Patrick's Day*	**18** 2nd ♌ ☽ v/c 11:19 am ☽ → ♍ 9:41 pm	**19** 2nd ♍	**○** 2nd ♍ ☽ v/c 11:22 am ☉ → ♈ 5:58 pm ☽ → ♎ 9:28 pm Full Moon 9:43 pm *Ostara* *Sun enters Aries* *Spring Equinox* *Storm Moon*
24 3rd ♏ ☽ v/c 10:24 pm	**25** 3rd ♏ ☽ → ♐ 2:06 am	**26** 3rd ♐ ☽ v/c 10:37 pm	**27** 3rd ♐ ☽ → ♑ 10:07 am
31 4th ≈ ☽ v/c 11:02 pm	**1**	**2**	**3**

Eastern Standard Time (EST) becomes Eastern Daylight Time (EDT) March 10

ZODIAC SIGNS				PLANETS	
♈ Aries	♌ Leo	♐ Sagittarius		☉ Sun	♃ Jupiter
♉ Taurus	♍ Virgo	♑ Capricorn		☽ Moon	♄ Saturn
♊ Gemini	♎ Libra	≈ Aquarius		☿ Mercury	♅ Uranus
♋ Cancer	♏ Scorpio	♓ Pisces		♀ Venus	♆ Neptune
				♂ Mars	♇ Pluto

MARCH 2019

TH	F	SA	NOTES
28	**1** 4th ♑	**2** 4th ♑ ☽ v/c 1:47 pm ☽ → ♒ 2:06 pm	
7 1st ♓ ☽ v/c 2:08 pm ☽ → ♈ 3:27 pm	**8** 1st ♈	**9** 1st ♈ ☽ v/c 12:14 pm	
14 1st ♊ ◑ 2nd Quarter 6:27 am ☽ v/c 8:30 am ☽ → ♋ 5:49 pm	**15** 2nd ♋	**16** 2nd ♋ ☽ v/c 2:03 pm ☽ → ♌ 8:57 pm	
21 3rd ♎	**22** 3rd ♎ ☽ v/c 2:10 pm ☽ → ♏ 10:16 pm	**23** 3rd ♏	
28 3rd ♑ ◑ 4th Quarter 12:10 am ☿ D 9:59 am *Mercury direct*	**29** 4th ♑ ☽ v/c 8:05 pm ☽ → ♒ 9:46 pm	**30** 4th ♒	
4	5	6	

APRIL 2019

SU	M	T	W
31	4th ≈ ☽ → ♓ 10:48 am **1**	4th ♓ **2**	4th ♓ ☽ v/c 11:36 am ☽ → ♈ 10:56 pm **3**
	All Fools' Day		
1st ♉ **7**	1st ♉ ☽ v/c 4:29 am ☽ → ♊ 5:15 pm **8**	1st ♊ **9**	1st ♊ ☽ v/c 1:27 pm ☽ → ♋ 11:31 pm **10**
2nd ♌ ☽ v/c 9:38 pm **14**	2nd ♌ ☽ → ♍ 6:14 am **15**	2nd ♍ **16**	2nd ♍ ☽ v/c 12:29 am ☽ → ♎ 7:22 am **17**
3rd ♏ ☽ v/c 12:00 am ☽ → ♐ 11:59 am **21**	3rd ♐ **22**	3rd ♐ ☽ v/c 7:44 am ☽ → ♑ 6:50 pm **23**	3rd ♑ **24**
	Earth Day		
4th ≈ ☽ v/c 5:44 am ☽ → ♓ 6:11 pm **28**	4th ♓ **29**	4th ♓ ☽ v/c 5:57 pm **30**	1
5	6	7	8

Eastern Daylight Time (EDT)

ZODIAC SIGNS

♈ Aries	♌ Leo	♐ Sagittarius
♉ Taurus	♍ Virgo	♑ Capricorn
♊ Gemini	♎ Libra	≈ Aquarius
♋ Cancer	♏ Scorpio	♓ Pisces

PLANETS

☉ Sun	♃ Jupiter
☽ Moon	♄ Saturn
☿ Mercury	♅ Uranus
♀ Venus	♆ Neptune
♂ Mars	♇ Pluto

APRIL 2019

TH	F	SA	NOTES
4th ♈ **4**	4th ♈ ● New Moon 4:50 am ☽ v/c 10:15 pm *New Moon*	1st ♈ **6** ☽ → ♉ 9:06 am	
1st ♋ **11**	1st ♋ ◑ 2nd Quarter 3:06 pm ☽ v/c 7:33 pm	2nd ♋ **13** ☽ → ♌ 3:50 am	
2nd ♎ **18**	2nd ♎ ○ ☽ v/c 7:12 am Full Moon 7:12 am ☽ → ♏ 8:41 am *Wind Moon*	3rd ♏ **20** ☉ → ♉ 4:55 am *Sun enters Taurus*	
3rd ♑ **25** ☽ v/c 3:48 pm	3rd ♑ ◑ ☽ → ♒ 5:27 am 4th Quarter 6:18 pm	4th ♒ **27**	
2	**3**	**4**	
9	**10**	**11**	

Aspects & Moon Phases

☌ Conjunction	0°	● New Moon	(1st Quarter)
⚹ Sextile	60°	◐ Waxing Moon	(2nd Quarter)
☐ Square	90°	○ Full Moon	(3rd Quarter)
△ Trine	120°	◑ Waning Moon	(4th Quarter)
⚻ Quincunx	150°		
☍ Opposition	180°		

MAY 2019

SU	M	T	W
28	29	30	**1** 4th ♓ ☽→♈ 6:24 am *Beltane*
5 1st ♉ ☽ v/c 11:10 am ☽→♊ 11:40 pm	**6** 1st ♊	**7** 1st ♊ ☽ v/c 7:50 pm	**8** 1st ♊ ☽→♋ 5:06 am
12 2nd ♌ ☽ v/c 8:24 am ☽→♍ 12:22 pm *Mother's Day*	**13** 2nd ♍	**14** 2nd ♍ ☽ v/c 1:19 pm ☽→♎ 2:51 pm	**15** 2nd ♎
19 3rd ♐	**20** 3rd ♐ ☽ v/c 1:05 pm	**21** 3rd ♐ ☽→♑ 3:56 am ☉→♊ 3:59 am *Sun enters Gemini*	**22** 3rd ♑ ☽ v/c 11:58 pm
26 3rd ♒ ☽→♓ 2:08 am 4th Quarter 12:34 pm	◑ **27** 4th ♓ *Memorial Day*	**28** 4th ♓ ☽ v/c 12:21 am ☽→♈ 2:32 pm	**29** 4th ♈
2	3	4	5

Eastern Daylight Time (EDT)

MAY 2019

TH	F	SA	NOTES
4th ♈ **2**	4th ♈ **3** ☽ v/c 4:47 am ☽ → ♉ 4:18 am	4th ♉ ● New Moon 6:45 pm *New Moon*	
1st ♋ **9** ☽ v/c 10:06 pm	1st ♋ **10** ☽ → ♌ 9:14 am	1st ♌ ◐ 2nd Quarter 9:12 pm	
2nd ♎ **16** ☽ v/c 5:37 am ☽ → ♏ 5:26 pm	2nd ♏ **17**	2nd ♏ ○ ☽ v/c 5:11 pm Full Moon 5:11 pm ☽ → ♐ 9:21 pm *Flower Moon*	
3rd ♑ **23** ☽ → ♒ 1:49 pm	3rd ♒ **24**	3rd ♒ **25** ☽ v/c 8:51 am	
4th ♈ **30** ☽ v/c 11:08 am	4th ♈ **31** ☽ → ♉ 12:43 am	1	
6	7	8	

JUNE 2019

SU	M	T	W
26	27	28	29
2 4th ♉ ☽ → ♊ 7:48 am	**27** ... **2** 4th ♊ New Moon 6:02 am ● *New Moon*	**4** 1st ♊ ☽ v/c 11:42 am ☽ → ♋ 12:17 pm	**5** 1st ♋
9 1st ♍	**10** 1st ♍ 2nd Quarter 1:59 am ◐ ☽ v/c 8:01 am ☽ → ♎ 8:29 pm	**11** 2nd ♎	**12** 2nd ♎ ☽ v/c 11:15 am
16 2nd ♐ *Father's Day*	**17** 2nd ♐ ☽ v/c 4:31 am Full Moon 4:31 am ○ ☽ → ♑ 12:13 pm *Strong Sun Moon*	**18** 3rd ♑	**19** 3rd ♑ ☽ v/c 7:19 am ☽ → ♒ 10:01 pm
23 3rd ♓	**24** 3rd ♓ ☽ v/c 7:10 pm ☽ → ♈ 10:38 pm	**25** 3rd ♈ 4th Quarter 5:46 am ◐	**26** 4th ♈
30 4th ♊	**1**	**2**	**3**

Eastern Daylight Time (EDT)

ZODIAC SIGNS

♈ Aries	♌ Leo	♐ Sagittarius
♉ Taurus	♍ Virgo	♑ Capricorn
♊ Gemini	♎ Libra	♒ Aquarius
♋ Cancer	♏ Scorpio	♓ Pisces

PLANETS

☉ Sun	♃ Jupiter
☽ Moon	♄ Saturn
☿ Mercury	♅ Uranus
♀ Venus	♆ Neptune
♂ Mars	♇ Pluto

JUNE 2019

TH	F	SA	NOTES
30	31	1 4th ♉ ☽ v/c 6:53 pm	
6 1st ♋ ☽ v/c 10:10 am ☽ → ♌ 3:16 pm	7 1st ♌	8 1st ♌ ☽ v/c 5:23 pm ☽ → ♍ 5:45 pm	
13 2nd ♎ ☽ → ♏ 12:02 am	14 2nd ♏ ☽ v/c 3:46 pm Flag Day	15 2nd ♏ ☽ → ♐ 5:03 am	
20 3rd ♒	21 3rd ♒ ☽ v/c 10:02 am ☉ → ♋ 11:54 am Litha Sun enters Cancer Summer Solstice	22 3rd ♒ ☽ → ♓ 10:01 am	
27 4th ♈ ☽ v/c 3:51 am ☽ → ♉ 9:32 am	28 4th ♉	29 4th ♉ ☽ v/c 2:38 pm ☽ → ♊ 5:09 pm	
4	5	6	

ASPECTS & MOON PHASES

☌ Conjunction	0°	● New Moon	(1st Quarter)
⚹ Sextile	60°	◑ Waxing Moon	(2nd Quarter)
▢ Square	90°	○ Full Moon	(3rd Quarter)
△ Trine	120°	◑ Waning Moon	(4th Quarter)
⚻ Quincunx	150°		
☍ Opposition	180°		

JULY 2019

SU	M	T	W
30	1 4th ♊ ☽ v/c 5:48 pm ☽ → ♋ 9:24 pm	1 4th ♋ New Moon 3:16 pm ● *New Moon* *Solar Eclipse*	3 1st ♋ ☽ v/c 10:25 am ☽ → ♌ 11:19 pm
7 1st ♍ ☽ v/c 12:50 pm ☿ R 7:14 pm *Mercury retrograde*	8 1st ♍ ☽ → ♎ 2:07 am	9 1st ♎ 2nd Quarter 6:55 am ◐ ☽ v/c 3:36 pm	10 2nd ♎ ☽ → ♏ 5:29 am
14 2nd ♐ ☽ → ♑ 7:05 pm	15 2nd ♑	16 2nd ♑ ☽ v/c 5:38 pm ○ Full Moon 5:38 pm *Blessing Moon* *Lunar Eclipse*	17 3rd ♑ ☽ → ♒ 5:19 am
21 3rd ♓	22 3rd ♓ ☽ v/c 4:34 am ☽ → ♈ 6:02 am ☉ → ♌ 10:50 pm *Sun enters Leo*	23 3rd ♈	24 3rd ♈ ☽ v/c 10:48 am ◑ ☽ → ♉ 5:42 pm 4th Quarter 9:18 pm
28 4th ♊ ☽ v/c 11:24 am	29 4th ♊ ☽ → ♋ 7:31 am	30 4th ♋ ☽ v/c 11:32 pm	31 4th ♋ ☽ → ♌ 9:18 am ● New Moon 11:12 pm ☿ D 11:58 pm *New Moon* *Mercury direct*
4	5	6	7

Eastern Daylight Time (EDT)

JULY 2019

TH		F		SA		NOTES
1st ♌	**4**	1st ♌ ☽ v/c 2:24 am	**5**	1st ♌ ☽ → ♍ 12:25 am	**6**	
Independence Day						
2nd ♏ ☽ v/c 8:28 pm	**11**	2nd ♏ ☽ → ♐ 11:05 am	**12**	2nd ♐ ☽ v/c 9:30 pm	**13**	
3rd ♒ ☽ v/c 11:53 am	**18**	3rd ♒ ☽ → ♓ 5:19 pm	**19**	3rd ♓	**20**	
4th ♉	**25**	4th ♉	**26**	4th ♉ ☽ v/c 12:28 am ☽ → ♊ 2:29 am	**27**	
	1		2		3	
	8		9		10	

ASPECTS & MOON PHASES

☌ Conjunction	0°	● New Moon	(1st Quarter)	
✶ Sextile	60°	◐ Waxing Moon	(2nd Quarter)	
☐ Square	90°	○ Full Moon	(3rd Quarter)	
△ Trine	120°	◑ Waning Moon	(4th Quarter)	
⚻ Quincunx	150°			
☍ Opposition	180°			

AUGUST 2019

SU	M	T	W
28	29	30	31
4 1st ♍ ☽ v/c 12:27 am ☽ → ♎ 9:30 am	5 1st ♎	6 1st ♎ ☽ v/c 3:36 am ☽ → ♏ 11:31 am	31 ● 1st ♏ 2nd Quarter 1:31 pm
11 2nd ♐ ☽ → ♑ 12:50 am	12 2nd ♑ ☽ v/c 6:11 pm	13 2nd ♑ ☽ → ♒ 11:35 am	14 2nd ♒
18 3rd ♓ ☽ → ♈ 12:33 pm	19 3rd ♈	20 3rd ♈	21 3rd ♈ ☽ v/c 12:06 am ☽ → ♉ 12:37 am
25 4th ♊ ☽ v/c 2:58 am ☽ → ♋ 5:05 pm	26 4th ♋	27 4th ♋ ☽ v/c 4:55 am ☽ → ♌ 7:53 pm	28 4th ♌ ☽ v/c 8:07 pm
1	2	3	4

Eastern Daylight Time (EDT)

ZODIAC SIGNS

♈ Aries	♌ Leo	♐ Sagittarius
♉ Taurus	♍ Virgo	♑ Capricorn
♊ Gemini	♎ Libra	♒ Aquarius
♋ Cancer	♏ Scorpio	♓ Pisces

PLANETS

☉ Sun	♃ Jupiter
☽ Moon	♄ Saturn
☿ Mercury	♅ Uranus
♀ Venus	♆ Neptune
♂ Mars	♇ Pluto

AUGUST 2019

TH	F	SA	NOTES
1st ♌ ☽ v/c 4:48 pm **1** Lammas	1st ♌ ☽ → ♍ 9:20 am **2**	1st ♍ **3**	
2nd ♏ ☽ v/c 10:58 am **8** ☽ → ♐ 4:35 pm	2nd ♐ **9**	2nd ♐ ☽ v/c 3:50 pm **10**	
2nd ♒ ◯ Full Moon 8:29 am ☽ v/c 9:02 pm ☽ → ♓ 11:49 pm Corn Moon	3rd ♓ **16**	3rd ♓ ☽ v/c 6:35 pm **17**	
3rd ♉ **22** ☽ v/c 5:33 pm	3rd ♉ ◑ ☉ → ♍ 6:02 am ☽ → ♊ 10:34 am 4th Quarter 10:56 am Sun enters Virgo	4th ♊ **24**	
4th ♌ **29** ☽ → ♍ 7:57 pm	4th ♍ ● New Moon 6:37 am New Moon	1st ♍ **31** ☽ v/c 4:46 am ☽ → ♎ 7:08 pm	
5	**6**	**7**	

Aspects & Moon Phases

☌ Conjunction	0°	● New Moon	(1st Quarter)
✶ Sextile	60°	◑ Waxing Moon	(2nd Quarter)
☐ Square	90°	◯ Full Moon	(3rd Quarter)
△ Trine	120°	◐ Waning Moon	(4th Quarter)
⊼ Quincunx	150°		
☍ Opposition	180°		

SEPTEMBER 2019

SU	M	T	W
1st ♎ **1**	1st ♎ **2** ☽ v/c 4:34 am ☽ → ♏ 7:35 pm *Labor Day*	1st ♏ **3**	1st ♏ **4** ☽ v/c 6:58 am ☽ → ♐ 11:08 pm
2nd ♑ **8**	2nd ♑ **9** ☽ v/c 4:30 am ☽ → ♒ 5:24 pm	2nd ♒ **10**	2nd ♒ **11** ☽ v/c 1:22 am
3rd ♈ **15**	3rd ♈ **16** ☽ v/c 12:03 pm	3rd ♈ **17** ☽ → ♉ 6:31 am	3rd ♉ **18**
4th ♊ **22** ☽ → ♋ 12:50 am	4th ♋ **23** ☉ → ♎ 3:50 am ☽ v/c 6:05 pm *Mabon* *Sun enters Libra* *Fall Equinox*	4th ♋ **24** ☽ → ♌ 5:19 am	4th ♌ **25** ☽ v/c 12:14 pm
1st ♎ **29** ☽ v/c 10:06 pm	1st ♎ **30** ☽ → ♏ 5:42 am	♊ *1*	*2*
6	*7*	*8*	*9*

Eastern Daylight Time (EDT)

ZODIAC SIGNS

♈ Aries	♌ Leo	♐ Sagittarius
♉ Taurus	♍ Virgo	♑ Capricorn
♊ Gemini	♎ Libra	♒ Aquarius
♋ Cancer	♏ Scorpio	♓ Pisces

PLANETS

☉ Sun	♃ Jupiter
☽ Moon	♄ Saturn
☿ Mercury	♅ Uranus
♀ Venus	♆ Neptune
♂ Mars	♇ Pluto

SEPTEMBER 2019

TH	F	SA	NOTES
1st ♐ ◗ 2nd Quarter 11:10 pm	2nd ♐ **6** ☽ v/c 12:03 pm	2nd ♐ **7** ☽ → ♑ 6:37 am	
2nd ♒ **12** ☽ → ♓ 5:52 am	2nd ♓ **13**	2nd ♓ ○ ☽ v/c 12:33 am Full Moon 12:33 am ☽ → ♈ 6:32 pm *Harvest Moon*	
3rd ♉ **19** ☽ v/c 9:57 am ☽ → ♊ 4:58 pm	3rd ♊ **20**	3rd ♊ ◑ ☽ v/c 10:41 pm 4th Quarter 10:41 pm	
4th ♌ **26** ☽ → ♍ 6:37 am	4th ♍ **27** ☽ v/c 11:58 pm	4th ♍ ● ☽ → ♎ 6:03 am New Moon 2:26 pm *New Moon*	
3	**4**	**5**	
10	**11**	**12**	

ASPECTS & MOON PHASES

☌ Conjunction	0°	● New Moon	(1st Quarter)
✷ Sextile	60°	◐ Waxing Moon	(2nd Quarter)
☐ Square	90°	○ Full Moon	(3rd Quarter)
△ Trine	120°	◑ Waning Moon	(4th Quarter)
⊼ Quincunx	150°		
☍ Opposition	180°		

OCTOBER 2019

SU	M	T	W
29	**30**	1st ♏ **1**	1st ♏ ☽ v/c 5:46 am ☽ → ♐ 7:44 am **2**
2nd ♑ **6** ☽ v/c 7:25 pm ☽ → ≈ 11:42 pm	2nd ≈ **7**	2nd ≈ **8** ☽ v/c 2:27 pm	2nd ≈ **9** ☽ → ♓ 12:05 pm
2nd ♈ Full Moon 5:08 pm ☽ v/c 5:59 pm ○	3rd ♈ **14** ☽ → ♉ 12:24 pm	3rd ♉ **15**	3rd ♉ **16** ☽ v/c 4:37 am ☽ → ♊ 10:30 pm
Blood Moon			
3rd ♋ **20**	3rd ♋ ☽ v/c 8:39 am 4th Quarter 8:39 am ☽ → ♌ 12:29 pm ◑	4th ♌ **22**	4th ♌ **23** ☽ v/c 5:14 am ⊙ → ♏ 1:20 pm ☽ → ♍ 3:29 pm
			Sun enters Scorpio
4th ♎ ☽ v/c 4:22 am ☽ → ♏ 4:29 pm New Moon 11:39 pm ●	1st ♏ **28**	1st ♏ **29** ☽ v/c 1:34 pm ☽ → ♐ 5:58 pm	1st ♐ **30**
New Moon			
3	**4**	**5**	**6**

Eastern Daylight Time (EDT)

OCTOBER 2019

TH	F	SA	NOTES
1st ♐ **3**	1st ♐ **4** ☽ v/c 3:34 am ☽ → ♑ 1:43 pm	1st ♑ **4** ◑ 2nd Quarter 12:47 pm	
2nd ♓ **10**	2nd ♓ **11** ☽ v/c 5:55 am	2nd ♓ **12** ☽ → ♈ 12:46 am	
3rd ♊ **17**	3rd ♊ **18** ☽ v/c 10:14 pm	3rd ♊ **19** ☽ → ♋ 6:43 am	
4th ♍ **24**	4th ♍ **25** ☽ v/c 9:00 am ☽ → ♎ 4:20 pm	4th ♎ **26**	
1st ♐ **31** ☽ v/c 10:30 am ☿ ℞ 11:41 am ☽ → ♑ 10:38 pm *Samhain* *Halloween* *Mercury retrograde*	*1*	*2*	
7	*8*	*9*	

NOVEMBER 2019

SU	M	T	W
27	28	29	30
3 1st ♑ ☽ v/c 1:46 am ☽ → ≈ 6:19 am *Daylight Saving Time ends at 2:00 am*	4 1st ≈ 2nd Quarter 5:23 am ◗	5 2nd ≈ ☽ v/c 9:37 am ☽ → ♓ 6:08 pm *Election Day (general)*	6 2nd ♓
10 2nd ♈ ☽ v/c 9:00 am ☽ → ♉ 6:18 pm	11 2nd ♉	12 2nd ♉ Full Moon 8:34 am ○ ☽ v/c 10:48 am *Mourning Moon*	13 3rd ♉ ☽ → ♊ 3:46 am
17 3rd ♋ ☽ v/c 3:14 pm ☽ → ♌ 4:57 pm	18 3rd ♌	19 3rd ♌ ☽ v/c 4:11 pm 4th Quarter 4:11 pm ◖ ☽ → ♍ 8:54 pm	20 4th ♍ ☿ D 2:12 pm *Mercury direct*
24 4th ♎ ☽ → ♏ 12:58 am	25 4th ♏ ☽ v/c 12:30 pm	26 4th ♏ ☽ → ♐ 3:11 am New Moon 10:06 am ● *New Moon*	27 1st ♐
1	2	3	4

Eastern Daylight Time (EDT) becomes Eastern Standard Time (EST) November 3

NOVEMBER 2019

TH	F	SA	NOTES
31	1st ♑ 1	1st ♑ 2	
2nd ♓ 7 ☽ v/c 8:13 pm	2nd ♓ 8 ☽ → ♈ 6:49 am	2nd ♈ 9	
3rd ♊ 14	3rd ♊ 15 ☽ v/c 6:40 am ☽ → ♋ 11:15 am	3rd ♋ 16	
4th ♍ 21 ☽ v/c 10:31 pm ☽ → ♎ 11:20 pm	4th ♎ 22 ☉ → ♐ 9:59 am *Sun enters Sagittarius*	4th ♎ 23 ☽ v/c 9:49 pm	
1st ♐ 28 ☽ v/c 5:50 am ☽ → ♑ 7:33 am *Thanksgiving Day*	1st ♑ 29 ☽ v/c 10:57 pm	1st ♑ 30 ☽ → ♒ 3:13 pm	
5	6	7	

Aspects & Moon Phases

☌ Conjunction	0°	● New Moon	(1st Quarter)
✶ Sextile	60°	◗ Waxing Moon	(2nd Quarter)
☐ Square	90°	○ Full Moon	(3rd Quarter)
△ Trine	120°	◖ Waning Moon	(4th Quarter)
⚻ Quincunx	150°		
☍ Opposition	180°		

DECEMBER 2019

SU	M	T	W
1st ≈ **1**	1st ≈ ☽ v/c 7:27 am **2**	1st ≈ ☽ → ♓ 2:11 am **3**	1st ♓ 2nd Quarter 1:58 am ◑
2nd ♈ ☽ → ♉ 2:29 am **8**	2nd ♉ ☽ v/c 8:13 pm **9**	2nd ♉ ☽ → ♊ 11:47 am **10**	2nd ♊ **11**
3rd ♌ **15**	3rd ♌ ☽ v/c 5:10 pm **16**	3rd ♌ ☽ → ♍ 2:16 am **17**	3rd ♍ 4th Quarter 11:57 pm ◐
4th ♏ ☽ v/c 10:27 pm **22**	4th ♏ ☽ → ♐ 11:34 am **23**	4th ♐ **24** *Christmas Eve*	4th ♐ ☽ v/c 6:18 am ☽ → ♑ 4:45 pm **25** *Christmas Day*
1st ≈ **29**	1st ≈ ☽ v/c 5:24 am ☽ → ♓ 10:41 am **30**	1st ♓ **31** *New Year's Eve*	I
5	6	7	8

Eastern Standard Time (EST)

ZODIAC SIGNS

♈ Aries	♌ Leo	♐ Sagittarius
♉ Taurus	♍ Virgo	♑ Capricorn
♊ Gemini	♎ Libra	≈ Aquarius
♋ Cancer	♏ Scorpio	♓ Pisces

PLANETS

☉ Sun	♃ Jupiter
☽ Moon	♄ Saturn
☿ Mercury	♅ Uranus
♀ Venus	♆ Neptune
♂ Mars	♇ Pluto

GET MORE AT LLEWELLYN.COM

Visit us online to browse hundreds of our books and decks, plus sign up to receive our e-newsletters and exclusive online offers.

- **Free tarot readings • Spell-a-Day • Moon phases**
- **Recipes, spells, and tips • Blogs • Encyclopedia**
- **Author interviews, articles, and upcoming events**

GET SOCIAL WITH LLEWELLYN

Find us on 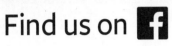 🐦 @LlewellynBooks

www.Facebook.com/LlewellynBooks

GET BOOKS AT LLEWELLYN

LLEWELLYN ORDERING INFORMATION

Order online: Visit our website at www.llewellyn.com to select your books and place an order on our secure server.

Order by phone:
- Call toll free within the US at 1-877-NEW-WRLD (1-877-639-9753)
- We accept VISA, MasterCard, American Express, and Discover.
- Canadian customers must use credit cards.

Order by mail:
Send the full price of your order (MN residents add 6.875% sales tax) in US funds plus postage and handling to: Llewellyn Worldwide, 2143 Wooddale Drive, Woodbury, MN 55125-2989

POSTAGE AND HANDLING

STANDARD (US):
(Please allow 12 business days)
$30.00 and under, add $6.00.
$30.01 and over, FREE SHIPPING.

INTERNATIONAL ORDERS, INCLUDING CANADA:
$16.00 for one book, plus $3.00 for each additional book.

Visit us online for more shipping options. Prices subject to change.

FREE CATALOG!

To order, call
1-877-
NEW-WRLD
ext. 8236
or visit our
website

DECEMBER 2019

TH	F	SA	NOTES
5 2nd ♓ ☽ v/c 3:15 am ☽ → ♈ 2:44 pm	**6** 2nd ♈	**7** 2nd ♈ ☽ v/c 10:01 am	
13 2nd ♊ ○ ☽ v/c 12:12 am Full Moon 12:12 am ☽ → ♋ 6:23 pm *Long Nights Moon*	**13** 3rd ♋	**14** 3rd ♋ ☽ v/c 10:57 am ☽ → ♌ 10:56 pm	
19 4th ♍ ☽ v/c 3:07 am ☽ → ♎ 5:04 am	**20** 4th ♎	**21** 4th ♎ ☽ v/c 6:45 am ☽ → ♏ 7:57 am ☉ → ♑ 11:19 pm *Yule Sun enters Capricorn Winter Solstice*	
26 4th ♑ ● New Moon 12:13 am *New Moon Solar Eclipse*	**27** 1st ♑ ☽ v/c 4:03 pm	**28** 1st ♑ ☽ → ♒ 12:21 am	
2	3	4	
9	10	11	

ASPECTS & MOON PHASES

☌ Conjunction	0°	● New Moon	(1st Quarter)
⚹ Sextile	60°	◑ Waxing Moon	(2nd Quarter)
□ Square	90°	○ Full Moon	(3rd Quarter)
△ Trine	120°	◐ Waning Moon	(4th Quarter)
⚻ Quincunx	150°		
☍ Opposition	180°		